Out of LONDON

The 60 Best Day Trips

Mary Peplow and Debra Shipley

ROBERT NICHOLSON PUBLICATIONS

A Nicholson Guide

First published 1989

© Robert Nicholson Publications 1989

Map
© Robert Nicholson Publications

Design by Bob Vickers
Cover artwork and line drawings by Joanna Canessa

Robert Nicholson Publications
16 Golden Square
London W1R 4BN

Typeset by Rowland Phototypesetting Ltd,
Bury St Edmunds, Suffolk
Printed in Great Britain by
Scotprint Ltd, Musselburgh

ISBN 0 948576 30 8

89/1/115

CONTENTS

4   **Contents**

FOREWORD

We have personally tried and tested all the day trips in this book, usually in the company of family or friends. The excursions are all very different but we have enjoyed every one of them and hope you do, too. When describing our various experiences we have tried to capture our impressions of the day – but of course you may have a different reaction and we would be interested to hear your views. Indeed, if you have any suggestions for other outings from London, please do write and tell us about them.

Mary Peplow and Debra Shipley are freelance feature and travel writers. They both live in London and have written many guide books together, including *London: The Good Tour Guide*, which is also published by Nicholson.

NB: Opening hours and facilities are subject to change without notice. It is always advisable to telephone and check the details before setting off to avoid disappointment.

AUDLEY END HOUSE AND GARDENS
43 miles NE

Whether you view it from the road or the gardens, from the front or the back, the splendour of this Jacobean country mansion is simply breathtaking. The original palace was built in 1603–16 by Thomas Howard when he was Lord Treasurer during the affluent days before his financial demise. What you see today is only a third of the original building but it's still one of the largest houses in the country and it's not just beautiful packaging either – you certainly won't be disappointed by the treasures within. A stunned silence usually falls over visitors as they stop in their tracks to admire the Great Hall with its exquisitely carved Jacobean wooden screen and contrasting early-18thC simple stone screen thought to be designed by Sir John Vanbrugh, playwright and architect. This is only the start and as you go from one splendidly decorated room to another, the house shows off its pictures, furniture and other details, all thoughtfully arranged in a very accessible manner. There are few ropes to bar the way and just the right number of attendants to be helpful without being imposing. Among the most popular rooms are the Little Drawing Room which is the work of Robert Adam; and Lord Braybrooke's Sitting Room which is a mini art gallery with paintings, including a pair of Van Goyen landscapes and Canaletto's famous *Venice*.

The concentration of riches and intimacy of detail in the house can be rather exhausting. Thankfully the surrounding 99-acre (40ha) park, landscaped by Lancelot 'Capability' Brown in 1762, is less mentally demanding, but you'll need to do some walking if you want to see it all. For the best overall view, it's worth making the effort to climb the hill at the rear of the house. Stand beside the now ruined Temple of Concord and see the grounds laid out before you, dotted with classical-style ornamental buildings and bridges. To the west of the house is the red brick Stables block which contains a small collection of latter-day agricultural machinery, old wagons and the estate fire engine. At the opposite end of the Stables Yard is the garden centre and farm shop selling fresh fruit, vegetables and plants grown on the estate. As you return, do stop and enjoy the view from the Stables Bridge. This awe-inspiring spectacle was carefully planned by Capability Brown to show the house in its full glory.

Practical details

Audley End House and Gardens, Audley End, Saffron Walden, Essex. (0799) 22399.

Open Apr–Oct grounds 12.00–17.00, house 13.00–17.00 Tue–Sun. Closed Mon except Bank Hols.
Admission charge (English Heritage).
Disabled facilities access to substantial ground floor area and gardens only.

Other facilities free car park, toilets, large gift shop, restaurant, picnic area, special events.
Rail Liverpool Street to Audley End (50mins).
Nearby Cambridge (12 miles), Knebworth (18 miles), Shuttleworth Collection (22 miles), Wimpole Hall (12 miles).

TREAT!

You're just a mile away from a seafood extravaganza at the Eight Bells public house in Saffron Walden. This black and white timbered pub was once the home of an Elizabethan wool merchant and the splendid old wool hall is now a restaurant full of charm and character with a menu to match.

Eight Bells, Bridge St. (0799) 22790.

TREAT!

AVEBURY STONE CIRCLES
80 miles SW

At sunset the summer landscape glows orange, the vibrant colour blotted out by rhythmically positioned black shapes; early morning, the black shapes now grey and seemingly crisp with sparkling late-autumn frosts; winter, austere and silent, the stones now shrouded in drifts of white snow; and finally spring, its green freshness adding yet another facet to the magic of Avebury Stone Circles. These are the changing faces of this site, but there are, however, five others which make up the whole Neolithic complex. They are West Kennet Avenue, The Sanctuary, West Kennet Long Barrow, Silbury Hill and Windmill Hill.

Avebury Stone Circles is the largest henge monument of its type in Britain and it's undoubtedly a charmed place which rarely fails to fire the imagination. The large outer circle and two inner circles, together with a surrounding ditch, cover some 28½ acres (11.5ha) and are impressive records of an ancient way of life. However, many of the stones are missing: where have they gone? Some have surely been used by local people to build farms, walls and houses, but many more have been destroyed or even buried! That tales of stones being shattered by lightning and of God's vengeance on this pagan site abound, comes as no surprise, but there's evidence to show that the dismantling of the circles and avenues has been a dangerous business throughout the ages. Apart from eight Neolithic burial sites found beside the megaliths, the body of 'barber-surgeon', as he became known, has also been discovered – the crushed skeleton of a medieval man complete with the tools of his trade.

Many of the majestically erect stones you can see today were exhumed during the excavation and restoration work carried out between 1925–9 by Alexander Keiller, heir to the Dundee marmalade fortune and keen archaeologist (it's well worth taking a look in

Avebury Museum founded by Keiller in 1938). His meticulous efforts both preserved the site and set a standard for the study of megaliths; it didn't solve the problem of their purpose, but it did provide the first indications as to how they might have been created. The stones, which are all sarsen, could have come from Marlborough Downs a few miles to the east. None of them have been hewn by man, and it would seem they have been selected for their shape which is either like a diamond, or thin with straight sides. To move the stones must have meant the use of ropes and some sort of sledge hauled by men, or possibly yoked oxen, and then erected with the help of wooden poles and more ropes. Although these stones must weigh up to 60 tonnes each, no pulleys or wheels were used. The experts agree that however the stones were assembled it must have taken enormous effort and energy to create this outstanding collection of monuments. As you visit each of the six sites you, too, will be amazed at the remaining evidence of such hard work.

Practical details

Avebury Stone Circles, 7 miles W of Marlborough, Wilts. Open any reasonable time. Free.

West Kennet Avenue, leading alongside B4003 from the stone circles. Open any reasonable time. Free.

The Sanctuary, Overton Hill, beside A4, ½ mile E of West Kennet. Open any reasonable time. Free.

West Kennet Long Barrow, ¾ mile SW of West Kennet. Open any reasonable time. Free.

Silbury Hill, 1 mile W of West Kennet on A4. Open any reasonable time. Free.

Windmill Hill, 1½ miles NW of Avebury. Open any reasonable time. Free.

Disabled facilities access to Avebury Stone Circles and West Kennet Avenue.

Other facilities toilets, car park, café and gift shop at Avebury Stone Circles. Car park at Silbury Hill.

Avebury Museum. (067 23) 250.

Open Apr–Sep 09.30–18.30 Mon–Sun; Oct–Mar 09.30–13.00, 14.00–16.00 Mon–Sat, 14.00–16.00 Sun.

Admission charge.

Disabled facilities access.
Other facilities education
room, toilets, car park.
No public transport

Nearby Bath (22 miles),
Hawk Conservancy (22
miles), Stourhead (20
miles).

TREAT!

A short drive away is the pretty market town of
Marlborough with its attractive Georgian fronted
buildings and wide main street. The town straddles
a former stage-coach route from London to Bath
and is today best known for its private school,
Marlborough College which was established in
1843. Queen Elizabeth I, William Shakespeare,
Oliver Cromwell, Samuel Pepys and Charles II are
all said to have visited Marlborough at one time or
another. One mile out of town, besides the A4, you
can visit the White Horse which was cut into the
hillside in 1804.

TREAT!

BATH
107 miles W

If you're visiting the elegant honey-coloured city of
Bath for the first time, it's a good idea to begin by
boarding an open-top bus (which starts from the bus
station in Manvers Street) to take a leisurely guided
tour. For one thing, it's an excellent way to see at close
range some of the rich architectural detail for which
Georgian Bath is famed. Bath's outstanding architecture includes the dramatic sweeping curve of Ionic
columns which form the Royal Crescent. No. 1 has
been furnished and decorated to show a typical 18thC
interior. A couple of minutes' walk away, via the
Circus – a beautiful circle of Georgian buildings – is the
Costume Museum which houses one of Britain's most
outstanding costume collections. Here, some 400 years

of style can be glimpsed through the distinctive dress of the flapper, dandy, beau and courtier along with a host of intimate items and personal accessories. By contrast, Bath Industrial Heritage Museum records a harsher side of the city; an aspect rarely considered by visitors. It shows the entire works of J. B. Bowler, a Victorian engineer and mineral water manufacturer, displayed as in the original premises – the detail is quite extraordinary.

However, the museum most people want to see, and indeed should not miss, is the Roman Baths and Pump Room where the city's two great heydays merge. It is here that natural hot springs bubble out of the ground at a constant 46.5°C and here between the 1st and 5th centuries AD that a bathing complex flourished in the Roman town of Aquae Sulis. A remarkable amount can still be seen today including swimming pools, saunas and Turkish baths. The hot springs became the vogue again during the 18thC and if you'd like to follow in fashionable footsteps try taking tea in the Georgian Pump Room. While in the vicinity of the Pump Room have a look around its neighbour – a 15thC abbey which has a lovely stone fan-vaulted Victorian nave. If time allows, make your way to the American Museum

Roman Baths and Abbey

a mile or so away at Claverton Manor. It has very little to do with Bath but the collection of some 18 furnished rooms is fascinating and well worth a visit. They illustrate American domestic life from the late 17th to 19th centuries and outside can be found a Conestoga wagon and a teepee.

Practical details

Tourist Information Centre, Abbey Church Yard. (0225) 462831. Open May–Sep 09.30–19.00 Mon–Sat, 10.00–16.00 Sun; Oct–Apr 09.30–17.00 Mon–Sat, closed Sun.

American Museum, Claverton Manor. (0225) 60503. Open Mar–Nov 14.00–17.00 Mon–Sun. Charge.

Bath Industrial Heritage Museum, Julian Rd. (0225) 318348. Open Feb–Nov 14.00–17.00 Mon–Sun; Dec–Jan 14.00–17.00 Sat & Sun only. Charge.

Bath Museum of Costume, Bennett St. (0225) 461111. Open Mar–Oct 09.30–17.30 Mon–Sat, 10.00–17.30 Sun; Nov–Feb 10.00–16.30 Mon–Sat; 11.00–16.30 Sun. Charge.

No. 1 Royal Crescent. (0225) 28126. Open

Mar–Dec 11.00–17.00 Tue–Sat, 14.00–17.00 Sun; Nov–Feb 14.00–16.00 Sat & Sun. Charge.

Roman Baths & Pump Room, Stall St. (0225) 461111. Open Mar–Oct 09.00–18.00 Mon–Sun (to 19.00 Jul & Aug); Nov–Feb 09.00–17.00 Mon–Sat, 10.00–16.00 Sun. Charge.

Rail Paddington to Bath Spa (1hr 40mins).

Coach National Express Victoria to Bath (2hrs 15mins).

Nearby Avebury (22 miles), Stourhead (15 miles), Westonbirt Arboretum (20 miles).

TREAT!

Built in 1480 and said to be the oldest house in Bath (a claim it upholds with the tiny museum in its cellar which boasts Roman and medieval foundations), Sally Lunn's is renowned for its buns. Sally came to Bath in 1680 and her bakery quickly became fashionable. Today, her buns are still baked on the premises to the original secret recipe and then topped with substantial savoury sauces, or smothered in jam and cream for the sweet toothed.

Sally Lunn's, 4 North Parade Passage. (0255) 61634. Open 10.00–18.00 Mon–Sat, 12.00–18.00 Sun. Museum open mornings only, closed Sun. Charge.

TREAT!

BATTLE ABBEY AND BATTLEFIELD
57 miles SE

1066 – the one date in history that everyone remembers. At 09.00 on Saturday 14 October 1066, a rousing blare of trumpets signalled the start of the now celebrated Battle of Hastings between the English army, led by King Harold, and the invading forces of William, Duke of Normandy. The field where the armies met in bitter conflict is open to the public and by walking around you can relive some of the drama of the day. Entrance to the battlefield is via the great gatehouse of Battle Abbey, a Benedictine abbey founded by William the Conqueror in celebration of his victory but also as penance for the many deaths incurred. Stand for a while and imagine the scene. You're on Senlac Hill, an advantageous position held by Harold. Each of William's desperate charges were countercharged until Harold went in pursuit and lost his hold on the hill. A series of special table models placed at strategic points helps to create a picture of the events of that momentous day; there is also an audio-visual programme on the battle in the Visitor Centre.

The tour of the battlefield, which is essentially a country walk up hills, through woods and across marshland, ends at the abbey ruins. The abbey was partially destroyed during the Dissolution in the 1530s.

The west range of the abbey cloisters is now a girls' school and not open to visitors but you can still see the site of the abbey church, the east range of cloisters and the undercroft of the former guest house. It was William's express wish that the high altar of the abbey should be built over the exact spot where King Harold fell, killed, legend has it, by an arrow in his eye. William's wish was granted, even though, as you'll discover, it meant the abbey had to be built on a slope. A stone now marks the site where Harold was slain.

Still on the theme of the Battle of Hastings, there's an excellent diorama in the town museum which really conjures up some of the tensions at the peak of the fighting. The museum also has a reproduction of the famous Bayeux Tapestry tracing the course of the battle.

Practical details

Battle Abbey and Battlefield, Battle, East Sussex. (042 46) 3792.

Open Apr–Sep 09.30–18.30 Mon–Sat, 14.00–18.30 Sun; Oct–Mar 09.30–16.00 Mon–Sat, 14.00–16.00 Sun.
Admission charge (English Heritage).
Disabled facilities access to abbey ruins only.
Other facilities car park, toilets, café nearby.
Battle Museum, Langton House, Battle Abbey Green. No tel number. Open Easter–Oct but hours vary.
Rail Charing Cross or Waterloo East to Battle (1hr 30mins).
Coach National Express Victoria to Battle (2hrs 15mins).
Nearby Drusillas (16 miles), Great Dixter House (8 miles), Rye and Winchelsea (12 miles).

TREAT!

Buckley's Museum of Shops, opposite the abbey wall, takes a look at the past – but not quite so far back as 1066. In fact, many older visitors to this museum of shopping and social habits will find the shopfronts and exhibits on display bring back nostalgic memories of the days of the corner shop. The museum gives a fascinating insight into shopping trends of yesteryear and among the shops represented are a chemist's, a pawnbroker's, a draper's and a toy shop. The goods on display are all appropriately priced.

Buckley's Museum of Shops, 90 High St. (042 46) 4269. Open Apr–Oct 10.00–17.30 Mon–Sun; Nov–Dec 10.00–17.30 Mon–Wed & Fri–Sun, closed Thur; Jan–Mar 10.00–17.30 Sat, Sun & school hols. Charge.

TREAT!

BEAULIEU
85 miles S

Beaulieu, which means 'the beautiful place', is the ancestral home of Lord and Lady Montagu. The crumbling remains of a Cistercian abbey cloister and the Palace House (once the gatehouse of Beaulieu Abbey itself) can still rightly be called beautiful, but much has changed.

Since Lord Montagu opened his home to the public in 1952 it has been developed into a major tourist attraction with a host of activities on offer. There's a short, and slightly disappointing, high-level monorail which circuits the complex, passing over vegetable plots and beside strange-looking domes which house an extensive model railway. Nearby, small radio-controlled cars can be raced and there's a miniature bike and car track. However, these are all secondary to Beaulieu's main attraction – the National Motor Museum.

No motor enthusiast could be disappointed with this outstanding collection, considered one of the finest and most comprehensive in the world, but there's also something here for all the family. One of the latest projects is 'Wheels' billed as 'a unique experience recalling the first hundred years of motoring'. You are

Beaulieu Palace House

firmly locked into seats and 'driven', with plenty of
swerves, through a time-capsule exhibition. You learn
about the development of the car from its uncomfort-
able pioneering days when hot water bottles were the
order of the day, right up to the latest moon buggy.
After this fascinating 'journey', it's time to take a look
at the collection itself which offers an enormous
amount to see. Favourites include the 1930 4½ litre
Supercharged Bentley and the MG Midget of the same
year. Then there's the popular Morris Minor which has
become a cherished collectors' item, and the 50s classic
Mercedes 300 SL which has a distinctive futuristic
appearance. The car which put a new word into the
English language – the Mini – is on show, together with
the Aston Martin DB5 once owned by Peter Sellers.
£1,000,000 was the price tag in 1960 for the 30ft long
Bluebird designed to break the World Land Speed
Record which it did on 17 July 1964, reaching
403.1mph.

Other vehicles on show include motorbikes, a red
London double-decker bus, bakery vans and fire engines along with perhaps the most exciting of all,
Grand Prix racing cars. You'll certainly wear your feet
out walking around the motors long before you've seen
all this gleaming and colourful museum has to offer.

Practical details

Beaulieu, Brockenhurst, Hants. (0590) 612345.

Open May–Sep 10.00–18.00 Mon–Sun; Oct–Apr 10.00–17.00 Mon–Sun. Closed Christmas Day.
Admission charge.
Disabled facilities access is limited to the ground floors only of the house and museum.
Other facilities Information Centre, variety of shops (selling gifts, books, kitchen equipment and herbs), restaurants, bars, toilets, first aid post, babycare, post box, telephone, readmission pass (available for use on day of admission only). Special events (historic car cavalcade, autojumble, car rallies) held throughout the year. Details from Special Events Dept. Dogs not allowed into any of the buildings or on monorail. *Note* not all facilities open during the winter months.
Rail Waterloo to Southampton (1hr) then bus, or Waterloo to Brockenhurst then taxi (six miles).
Nearby Broadlands (16 miles), New Forest (2 miles), Poole (24 miles).

TREAT!

Just 2½ miles walk through woodland and beside Beaulieu River is Buckler's Hard with its attractively positioned and unusual museum. The main part of the museum is devoted to an informative maritime exhibition reflecting the maritime history of the village. (This is where ships for Nelson's fleet were built.) In addition to the museum you should also visit the main street of the pretty 18thC settlement which has been preserved. Behind the small cottage façades there's a whole village world to discover. You can also take a river trip during the summer season on the catamaran *Swiftsure* and sip a cocktail or two in style.

The Maritime Museum, Buckler's Hard (signposted from Beaulieu). (059 063) 203. Open Easter–Spring Bank Holiday 10.00–18.00 Mon–Sun;

Spring Bank Holiday–Sep 10.00–21.00 Mon–Sun;
Oct–Easter   10.00–16.30   Mon–Sun.   Closed
Christmas Day.

TREAT!

BEKONSCOT MODEL VILLAGE
23 miles W

There's a dreamlike quality to this model village, a
miniature wonderland set in the 1930s, where visitors
tower like Gulliver over the kingdom of small people.
Bekonscot claims to be the oldest model village in the
world. It is the masterpiece of Roland Callingham, an
accountant with the all-consuming hobby of model-
making. He created Bekonscot in the 1920s in a field
opposite his home, choosing the name as a mixture of
Beaconsfield where he was living, and Ascot which was
his former home.

Set in a delightful rock garden with some 5000
different shrubs and conifers, the village has expanded
since it was first opened to the public in 1929. The
circuitous route now takes you past shops, streets,
houses, lakes, a school, fairground, zoo, farm and
football pitch; there are even a coal-mine and race
track among the other, more typical, features of everyday life in a 1930s village. You can see the cricket team
playing and the children running around on the green.
It's market day at Splashynge and the Morris Dancers
with musical accompaniment are in full swing. The
blacksmith is working at his anvil, locals are drinking
outside the Grantley Arms and the cinema is showing
Snow White and the Seven Dwarfs. The real pride of
Bekonscot, however, is the model railway which
travels around the village, the trains appearing at the
most unexpected moments as they hurtle on to the next
station. There are seven stations in all with the signal
box at Maryloo Station to control and supervise the
operation.

Visitors are asked to follow a set route along a

narrow path through and around the village. This does ensure you won't miss anything, but also means that on busy days the queue can be rather slow-moving with everyone keen to take everything in and photographers making the most of opportunities for unusual shots. You may have to exercise extra patience but it's surprising what you discover if you take your time and look carefully. The detailing is immaculate and the scenes full of imagination. There are some nice touches of humour, too, which always raise a smile even if the children do insist on going around again and again.

Practical details

Bekonscot Model Village, Warwick Rd, Beaconsfield, Bucks. (0494) 672919.

Open Mar–Oct 10.00–17.00 Mon–Sun. Trains run Apr–Oct.
Admission charge.
Disabled facilities access limited to wheelchairs under 21" (53.3cm) wide (suitable wheelchairs available for loan on site).
Other facilities free car park, toilets, gift shop, refreshment kiosk and picnic areas, rain shelter, children's playground.
Rail Marylebone to Beaconsfield (43mins).
Coach Green Line Victoria to Beaconsfield (1hr 20mins).
Nearby Hughenden Manor (8 miles), Thorpe Park (16 miles), Windsor (10 miles).

TREAT!

Follow the signs to Wooburn Green and you'll come to a lovely picnic spot with benches and tables. Bordering on the Burnham Beeches, it also gives easy access to scenic drives and walks through this woodland famed for its beech trees. Many of these are well over 400 years old and are as gnarled and warped as befits such a venerable age.

TREAT!

BIRDWORLD AND UNDERWATER WORLD
30 miles SW

Situated on the edge of Alice Holt Forest, the lovely gardens of Birdworld make an attractive home for a variety of birds of all shapes and sizes from the tiny ruby humming bird to the huge ostrich. As you might imagine, it's a delight for photographers and artists but Birdworld is especially popular with small children, who never seem to tire of watching the pelicans catching fish in their beaks, or the parrots tucking into the 'macaw fruit feed' which can be bought from the gift shop. And to help parents and teachers plan the day, the grounds are extremely well laid out with plenty of information plaques giving details of the different birds.

During the summer season (Apr–Aug), there's a 'Safari Ride' (extra charge) which transports visitors

Parrots, Birdworld

around the bird enclosures and gives more detail about each species. But the best way to enjoy Birdworld is definitely on foot. There is a suggested route around the planted aviaries and enclosures, but you're free to roam around as you like, returning to take a look at your favourite birds whenever you feel like it. And every visitor does seem to have a particular favourite – whether it's the ostrich, the largest bird in the world, the cockatoo or the expertly camouflaged tawny owl. Penguin Island is an extremely popular attraction. This 20,000-gallon glass-fronted tank is specially designed so that visitors can watch as the penguins dive and swim around the island – and it certainly makes a lively sight. Feeding times at 11.30 and 15.30 provide the best spectacle. Something else not to be missed is the Seashore Walk, an area re-created as a seashore complete with waves, the wreck of a fishing boat and, of course, many kinds of seabirds.

Next door to Birdworld is Underwater World, a large indoor aquarium with an amazing collection of tropical fish. Many of the fish – such as the highly coloured clown fish, the huge pacu and, lurking somewhere, the ferocious piranha – can be seen immediately but the secret is to stand back, wait awhile and slowly let the other fish come into view – each one a different shape and many covered with intricate patterns. Underwater World and Birdworld can be visited separately but the two combine to offer a really interesting and enjoyable outing.

Practical details

Birdworld and Underwater World, Holt Pound, Farnham, Surrey. (0420) 22140.

Open Apr–Aug
09.30–18.00 Mon–Sun;
Sep 09.30–17.00
Mon–Sun; Oct–Mar
09.30–15.30 Mon–Sun.
Admission charge.
Disabled facilities
unlimited access.

Other facilities free car park, toilets, gift shop, café and picnic places, children's play area, fun and fitness trail. No dogs or pets allowed.
Rail Waterloo to
Aldershot (45mins) and

then bus to Birdworld (15mins).
Coach Green Line Victoria direct (2hrs). Runs Apr–Sep, Sat & Sun only.

Nearby Loseley House (12 miles), Winchester (25 miles), Wisley (20 miles).

TREAT!

Anyone interested in birds and natural history will also enjoy a visit to the nearby village of Selbourne. It was here that the 18thC naturalist and founder of modern ornithology, the Reverend Gilbert White, kept a record of the local wildlife which was published in 1789 as *The Natural History and Antiquities of Selbourne*. His old home 'The Wakes' is now two museums, one devoted to the life and works of White himself, and the other to two great explorers – the 19thC naturalist Frank Oates and his nephew Captain Lawrence Oates, who took part in Scott's famous expedition to the Antarctic. Outside, the garden is planted in 18thC style and is a delight to wander around. If time allows do take a stroll around the lovely village and, for a beautiful view, climb the zig-zag path which White helped to make to the top of the beech woods of Selbourne Hanger.

Gilbert White Museum and The Oates Memorial Library and Museum, The Wakes, Selbourne, Alton, Hants. (042 050) 275. Open Mar–Oct 12.00–17.30 (last admission 17.00) Tue–Sun. Charge.

TREAT!

BLENHEIM PALACE
63 miles E

Known as the birthplace of wartime Prime Minister Sir Winston Churchill, Blenheim Palace is an enormously popular tourist destination. Here you can see a host of memorabilia associated with this renowned politician, including the room in which he was born, his childhood curls, numerous photographs and an exhibition charting his life and work.

Blenheim is also interesting architecturally. Designed by Sir John Vanbrugh and completed in 1719, the palace is considered one of the best examples of English baroque in the country; the north front is particularly fine. Once inside the first impression is of heavy grandeur. The Great Hall, which towers some 67ft (20.4m) high, has a remarkable Thornhill ceiling with carved stone embellishments by Grinling Gibbons – look out for the arms of Queen Anne on the keystone of the main arch which spans the Minstrels' Gallery. From the Great Hall you will be guided through the various rooms open to the public. They include the Green Drawing Room which retains its original ceiling by Nicholas Hawksmoor, the Red Drawing Room with a painting by Sir Joshua Reynolds, and the Green Writing Room where the tapestry of the Duke of Marlborough accepting Marshall Tallard's surrender at the Battle of Blenheim (1704) is on display. You are also shown into the astonishing Saloon. This is the State Dining Room and it is still used by the family once a year on Christmas Day. Its walls are covered in murals by Louis Laguerre (1663–1721). All sorts of people are caricatured between painted classical columns including the artist himself who stands beside Dean Jones, Marlborough's chaplain. Three State Rooms lead off from the Saloon. The walls of all three are hung with tapestries of Marlborough's campaigns.

Blenheim Palace

The rich gilded woodwork of the State Rooms is late 19thC in date, but is modelled by highly skilled French craftsmen who are thought to have copied the boiseries of Louis XVI's bedroom. The guided tour ends in the Long Library (180ft – 54.9m – long), but you are then free to visit the chapel and wander through the grounds. There are water terraces, a walled kitchen garden and a formal Italian Garden, but most impressive of all is the parkland and beautiful lake created by Capability Brown.

Practical details

Blenheim Palace, Woodstock, Oxon. (0993) 811325.

Open mid Mar–end Oct 10.30–18.00 (last admission 17.00) Mon–Sun. Park open all year 09.00–18.00. Closed Christmas Day.
Admission charge.
Disabled facilities access good throughout.

Other facilities café, restaurant, picnic, shop, toilets, car park.
No public transport
Nearby Cotswold Wild Life Park (18 miles), Oxford (10 miles).

TREAT!

The Bear Hotel in Woodstock is said to have been old when Blenheim Palace was new. Many original features survive from its coaching inn past including massive oak beams and a 16thC staircase. These, along with a large open fireplace, make The Bear a pleasant place to visit for a drink. You may even be tempted to have a meal. The Bear's restaurant has a reputation for both table d'hôte and à la carte menus and boasts an extensive wine list. Not surprisingly it is popular so advance booking is essential, and unfortunately very little time is allowed to linger after a meal as service is in two sittings.

The Bear Hotel, Park St. (0993) 811511.

TREAT!

THE BLUEBELL RAILWAY
46 miles S

A whistle, a puff of smoke and you're back in a bygone age when ladies wore bonnets and the sun was always shining. For the older generation the Bluebell Railway is a chance to reminisce and exchange travelling tales; for youngsters it's an exciting outing with a difference. For everyone it's an experience not to be missed. Opened in 1960, the first of the disused steam passenger lines to be restored to working order, the Bluebell Railway runs along a five-mile stretch of a former British Railways branch line between Sheffield Park and Horsted Keynes. Single or return tickets can be bought at either station, but most people choose to set off from Sheffield Park and make a round trip of it.

From the moment you walk through the entrance of Sheffield Park Station, the journey back into the age of steam begins. The station has been restored in the late-Victorian style of the London, Brighton and South Coast Railway with remarkable old-style signals and a signal box complete with polished dials and painted levers. Small touches, like the trunk waiting to be loaded onto a train, add to the authenticity. There's plenty to see as well – displays of vintage enamel advertisements, and a museum on Platform 2 which is small but packed with signs, models, tickets and other relics which help build up the story of the line and the men who worked on it. You're also welcome to browse around the engine shed and take a closer look at the historic locomotives, coaches and wagons. The railway has 30 locomotives, 6 of which are over 100 years old. Steam enthusiasts will be able to identify the different designs and fully appreciate the rather complicated potted histories on the information plaques. For those less 'in the know', the sight of the magnificent veteran locomotives is still quite breathtaking.

However, the highlight is definitely the actual journey aboard the historic coaches, painstakingly restored

Bluebell Railway, Sheffield Park Station

both inside and out with attention given to every small detail. The trip to Horsted Keynes, now re-created in the elegant 1930s style of the Southern Railway, takes about 15 minutes. The train moves at a leisurely pace through the rolling countryside of the Sussex Weald, so try to get a seat at the front and watch as cows raise their heads occasionally to stare as you pass and clouds of smoke drift behind. The scenery is spectacular throughout the season, but travellers in the spring can catch a glimpse of the unforgettable sight that gave the Bluebell Railway its name – the carpet of blue flowers on either side of the line.

Practical details

The Bluebell Railway, Sheffield Park Station, Nr Uckfield, East Sussex. (082 572) 2370 (24hr train information), (082 572) 3777 (bookings and enquiries).

Open Jun–Sep, Mon–Sun; Mar–May & Oct–Dec, Sat & Sun; Jan–Feb, Sun only; most school hols & Bank Hols. Please phone for individual train times. *Admission* charge.

Disabled facilities good but contact in advance. *Other facilities* free car park, toilets, well-stocked gift shop, café and picnic areas at both stations, special events.

Rail Victoria to Haywards Heath (1hr) then connecting bus or coach (30mins).
Coach National Express Victoria to Sheffield Park (1hr 45mins). London Country/Green Line Thornton Heath to Sheffield Park (1hr 45mins).
Nearby Hever Castle (16 miles), Penshurst Vineyards (15 miles), South Downs Way (16 miles).

TREAT!

Just two miles south of East Grinstead is a very welcoming and friendly stately home where everyone will enjoy a visit. Standen, a large family house of the 1890s, was designed by Philip Webb, a friend and associate of William Morris whose distinctive designs fill every room. It has been well restored and is complete in every detail including the original electric light fittings. Outside, there's a lovely hillside garden with very good views.

Standen, Nr East Grinstead, West Sussex. (0342) 23029. Open Apr–Oct 13.30–17.30 (last admission 17.00) Wed–Sun. Gardens open 12.30. Charge (National Trust).

TREAT!

BOULOGNE
120 miles SE

Many British day trippers cross the Channel to Boulogne only to board a waiting bus and travel immediately to one of the town's huge hypermarkets where they spend the whole day stocking up on beer and wine. The French have tales to tell of trippers staggering with more bottles than they could carry and finally dropping them – usually while crossing a road. There's even a story of a bus being so overloaded with alcohol that its bottom dropped out! If this is not your idea of having a good time, be different, give the hypermarket a miss, and make for the town itself.

Start by visiting the Tourist Information Bureau at the harbour (it has English-speaking representatives) where you can pick up a free town plan. Armed with this you will easily be able to explore Boulogne and discover some of its delicious specialist food shops. Make first for the area around Place Dalton which is the site of a colourful and bustling produce market. Nearby is La Fromagerie de Philippe Oliver; your quivering nose will lead you to it and tell you when you've arrived. A visit to Philippe's partially candle-lit shop, where some 150 different kinds of cheese are temptingly displayed, is something to savour. Cheese Master and total enthusiast, Philippe spends most of his holidays travelling France and Europe in search of the unusual and the tasty – and he certainly succeeds. For those with a sweet tooth there are plenty of pastry and fondant shops. Try André Lugand's Pâtisserie, where you can also rest and have a coffee or a luxurious hot chocolate. In the same street you can purchase beautifully wrapped scent from a traditional perfumery or buy some unusual dried fruits.

Shopping completed it's time to go sightseeing, so walk up the hill (5–10 minutes) to the pretty Old Town. Dominated by its cathedral, the Old Town offers a complete contrast to the commercial face of Boulogne over which it towers. The shops here, although pretty, cannot really be recommended; instead, walk the 13thC ramparts and take a look at the bell tower where the Count of Boulogne once kept his prisoners. You can also look at the castle exterior, and the cathedral (permission can sometimes be obtained to climb up into its dome), and generally soak up the atmosphere.

By now your day will be almost over and you should return to the commercial part of town. If you want to buy wine, now is the time. One of the best places to stock up is Le Chais. In this cellar you can taste before you buy and the selection is good. For beer, try a supermarket (there are several by the harbour), or a department store like Prisunic.

Take a few minutes for one last, lingering cup of coffee on French soil – try Bar Hamiot, it's quite an experience – and then it's off home with happy memories and shopping bags full of authentic French produce.

Practical details

Office de Tourisme, Pont Marguet. (33 21) 31 68 38. Open 10.00–12.00 & 14.00–19.00 Mon–Sun.

André Lugand, Pâtisserie, 9 Grande Rue. (33 21) 31 56 22.

Le Chais, 49 Rue des deux Ponts. (33 21) 31 65 42.

Indris (dried fruits), 24 Grande Rue. (33 21) 30 54 59.

Perfumerie Gilliocq, 6 Grande Rue. (33 21) 31 43 68.

Philippe Oliver, La Fromagerie, Rue Thiers. (33 21) 31 94 74.

Prisunic, 39 Rue de la Lampe. (33 31) 31 33 10.

Note French shops are open 09.00–12.00 & 14.00–19.00 Tue–Sat. Good buys include wine, cheese, mustard, kitchen utensils, pâté, walnut or olive oil, glasses, cooked meats (in sealed wrapping for export), wine and beer.

Cathedral, Rue de Lille. Open all the time. Crypt (contains the cathedral's treasure) open 09.00–12.00 Mon, Wed–Sun, 14.00–17.00 Tue–Sun.

Place Dalton market open 07.00–13.00 Wed & Sat.

Rail Charing Cross to Dover Priory (1hr 30mins) and then local train, taxi or bus to Dover Western Docks, or Victoria to Dover Priory (1hr 45mins) which then goes on to Dover Western Docks Station. Enquiries (01) 928 5100.

Coach National Express Victoria to Pencester Rd, Dover (2hrs 45mins) which then goes on to Eastern Docks. (The ferries go from Eastern Docks. The Hoverspeed and Jetfoil go from Western Docks. To get to Western Docks it is best to change to a local bus at Pencester Rd as it is a long walk between Eastern and Western Docks.) Enquiries (01) 730 0202.

Car London–Dover 75 miles. Parking at Dover (expensive). Motoring information (0634) 8021.

Hovercraft Hoverspeed International Hoverport, Western Docks (0304) 214514. Dover to Boulogne (40mins). Duty free facilities.

Note remember to take your passport.

```
┌─ TREAT! ───────────────────────────────┐
│                                          │
│  At some time during the day your stomach will │
│  demand food. You could try one of Boulogne's │
│  restaurants but if it's a fine day why not have a │
│  French-style picnic. Warm crusty bread, fresh │
│  fruit, some pâté, olives and of course a bottle or so │
│  of wine – all bought locally – should do the trick. A │
│  lovely spot to eat can be found just behind the │
│  cathedral where there are plenty of benches and │
│  lawns protected from the wind by the two ram- │
│  parts. The views are wonderful – all the way to │
│  Dover on a clear day.                   │
│                                          │
│                            _ TREAT! _    │
└──────────────────────────────────────────┘
```

BRIGHTON
56 miles S

Brighton can honestly boast something for all tastes. It's a major conference centre, a fun place for family holidays, a university town, and an excellent place for a day trip – the only problem is that you can't see all there is to see in a day!

Brighton Pier, built in 1899 and extending some 872yds (800m) into the sea, is just the place to prom- enade. Not only does it offer gentle, though often bracing, exercise it also provides perhaps the best views of Brighton's grand sea-front sweep of Regency architecture. Behind these impressive buildings you can discover a different Brighton; a place of quaint shops, maze-like passages, narrow lanes and intriguing arcades full of antiques and curiosities. However, for a bargain, you might like to try your luck at the Saturday street market which has over 100 stalls, all of them crammed with jewellery, silver, medals, coins, books, porcelain and furniture. To test your knowledge of antiques, or perhaps to learn a thing or two, pay a visit to Brighton Museum and Art Gallery – it has an exceptionally good collection of late 19th and early 20thC furniture.

Brighton Museum is housed in what were once the stables of the Royal Pavilion; it was royalty who made the town into a popular resort and the Pavilion, which was designed for the Prince of Wales, remains Brighton's most famous landmark. The prince (later to be King George IV) first visited Brighton in 1783 to sample the beneficial effects of the sea air so extolled by one Dr Richard Russell. The Pavilion was designed, as a classical building with a rotunda and dome, by Henry Holland in 1787. Later, in 1815 when the prince was Regent, John Nash was commissioned to redesign it. Nash, the architect of London's Regent's Park, added tent-like roofs, pretty pinnacles, and the distinctive, large onion-shaped dome which can be seen today. The exterior of the Pavilion is surprising enough, but the sumptuous interior is quite exquisite. Its lavish decoration includes a breathtaking Banqueting Room dominated by a huge, winged, silver dragon; a Saloon which houses an unusual couch made in the shape of an Egyptian river boat on crocodile feet; and, most spectacular and magical of all, the Music Room which is an undoubted masterpiece.

For a real contrast to the sizzling splendour of the Pavilion, round off your day in Brighton with a visit to the less spectacular but still impressive Preston Manor.

Royal Pavilion

Fully and thoughtfully furnished, Preston Manor illustrates the solid, secure way of life for a rich Brighton family in the years before the First World War.

Practical details

Brighton Tourism and Resort Services Department, Marlborough House, 54 Old Steine. (0273) 23755. Open 09.00–17.00 Mon–Sat.

Brighton Museum and Art Gallery, Church St. (0273) 603005. Open 10.00–17.45 Tue–Sat, 14.00–17.00 Sun. Free.

Brighton Pier. (0273) 609631. Open during daylight hours Mon–Sun. Free.

Brighton Street Market, Upper Gardener St. Open 07.00–13.00 Sat.

Preston Manor, Preston Park. (0273) 603005. Open 10.00–17.00 Tue–Sun & Bank Hol Mons. Charge.

The Royal Pavilion, Pavilion Estate. (0273) 603005. Open Jun–Sep 10.00–18.00 Mon–Sun; Oct–May 10.00–17.00 Mon–Sun. Charge.

Rail Victoria to Brighton (1hr 10mins).

Coach National Express Victoria to Brighton (2hrs 30mins).

Nearby Arundel (12 miles), Bluebell Railway (16 miles), Butlin's Southcoast World (25 miles), Drusillas (15 miles).

TREAT!

There are many tempting places to have a tasty meal in Brighton and, particularly if you like garlic, there are numerous small bistro-type restaurants. However, for an English-style tea with home-made cakes head for the Mock Turtle. It's tucked away, rather inauspiciously behind the bus station, but it's well worth seeking out. The fresh cream meringues are particularly recommended – they're huge!

The Mock Turtle Tea Shop, 4 Pool Valley. (0273) 27380. Open 10.00–18.00 Tue–Sat.

TREAT!

BROADLANDS
77 miles S

To visit Broadlands, an elegant Palladian-style house, is to follow in the footsteps of many distinguished people. The Queen and Prince Philip began their honeymoon here in 1947, as did Lord and Lady Louis Mountbatten in 1922. In 1981, the Prince and Princess of Wales also stayed for a few days after their wedding and just a few years earlier, in 1979, royal guests from all over the world gathered at Broadlands to celebrate Lord and Lady Romsey's wedding. Fittingly, you can see crown jewels of the world at Broadlands – albeit in perfect facsimile!

The Romseys took over Broadlands in 1979 after Lord Mountbatten's assassination. In his memory they have created, in the William and Mary stable building, an interesting Mountbatten Exhibition which highlights this important man's life. An informative, audio-visual presentation provides an excellent introduction to this sailor, military commander, statesman, diplomat, sportsman and inventor. Then there's a chance to see the large collection of his uniforms and decorations, trophies and gifts, mementoes and personal photographs.

In 1736, Lord Palmerston said of Broadlands '. . . this place altogether pleases me above any place I know' and many visitors over the years have found themselves in agreement with him. The original manor and area known as Broadlands was owned by Romsey Abbey from pre-Norman times. After the Dissolution of the Monasteries by Henry VIII in the 1530s, it was leased to private owners. The 'transformation' into the fine mid-Georgian building which can be seen today began much later, in 1767. Architect and landscape designer Capability Brown was commissioned by the second Viscount Palmerston to deformalise the earlier Tudor/Jacobean manor and its gardens. The result, a beautiful house set in a gentle landscape which seems to melt into the River Test, is said to be one of Capability Brown's greatest masterpieces.

The interior is just as attractive and interesting; the Domed Hall, Sculpture Hall, Drawing Room, Wedgwood Room, Library, Chinese Room and Wolfsgarten Room all seem to have a tale to tell. For example, the Wolfsgarten Room takes its name from the Summer Palace of the Grand Dukes of Hesse and the Rhine (recalling Lord Mountbatten's German ancestry) where wolves used to be kept to guard the gates.

Sir Winston Churchill once said 'we shape our buildings and then they shape us!' – something which might indeed be said of Broadlands with its history of great design and great statesmen.

Practical details

Broadlands, Romsey, Hants. (0794) 516878.

Open Apr–Sep 10.00–17.00 Tue–Sun & Bank Hol Mons.
Admission charge.
Disabled facilities access good to the Imperial Collection and Crown Jewels, and to the grounds; access to ground floor only of house and Mountbatten Exhibition.

Other facilities two shops, restaurant, toilets, free parking.
Rail Waterloo to Southampton (1hr) then Southampton to Romsey (12mins). For details of Romsey train phone (0794) 516878.
Nearby Beaulieu (16 miles), New Forest (10 miles), Salisbury (16 miles), Winchester (10 miles).

TREAT!

Throughout the year you can rent a pretty, self-catering, thatched cottage on the Broadlands estate – so why not treat yourself to a break? Enquiries and reservations can be made through Hideaways, 6 Bridge St, Salisbury. (0722) 24868.

TREAT!

BUTLIN'S SOUTHCOAST WORLD
60 miles SE

Thousands of families spend their annual break in the traditional holiday camp environment created at Butlin's Southcoast World. Billeted in a purpose-built 'village', these temporary residents share their entertainment facilities with thousands more families who visit just for the day. It's a concrete-block world designed to pack in as many people as possible. However, no one seems to mind the slightly run-down feel of Butlin's, nor its intrinsic ugliness – there's just too much going on. All the fun of the fair for a flat-price entrance fee, that's the great advantage of a day out at Southcoast World. Family favourites include dodgem cars, the colourful carousel and tummy-churning waltzer; other, more adventurous, rides can be judged for effectiveness by the loudness of the screams from those on board!

Another major attraction is Aquasplash – a steaming water complex of wave makers, slides and three dramatic flumes. On a cascade of water, and inside a huge coiling yellow tube, the flume takes the swimmer on an exhilarating ride which ends in a big splash. One drawback, though, is that Aquasplash is very popular, so its use is regulated into sessions and you may have to wait a while for your turn. Older visitors are entertained with cabaret, theatre shows and films. There are also facilities to play table tennis, badminton, indoor bowls and darts, though once again there are often queues and you may have to wait before taking part. If you're feeling energetic, you might like to flex a muscle and take out a rowing boat while the not so energetic might prefer to opt for a gentle game of putting.

Wherever you are on the complex, you are likely to come across the ever-helpful, and now legendary, 'Redcoats'. Yes, they really do still exist but disappointingly they are not rushing around organising the jolly japes and whacky contests that have come to be associated with their name. These attractions do not seem to be on offer to the day-tripper but, probably more useful, the Redcoats do have winning ways with children, and there is so much to do that Butlin's remains an ideal outing for a family.

Practical details

Butlin's Southcoast World, Bognor Regis, West Sussex. (0243) 822445.

Open Apr–Oct 10.00–19.30 Mon–Sun.
Admission charge.
Disabled facilities access about 80%.
Other facilities café, restaurant, picnic area, car parking, shop, toilets.

Rail Victoria to Bognor Regis (1hr 30mins).
Nearby Goodwood (8 miles), Weald and Downland Open Air Museum (10 miles), Wildfowl Trust, Arundel (15 miles).

TREAT!

The beach at Bognor is only a short walk away, but travelling by train is far more fun. A colourful mini-railway leaves from the camp at regular intervals to take you on a half-mile trip along the seafront to the Bognor Regis Centre.

No need to book. Charge.

TREAT!

CAMBRIDGE COLLEGES
60 miles N

'We were walking the whole time – out of one college into another . . . I felt I could live and die in them and never wish to speak again.' This was how Mary, wife of the essayist Charles Lamb, described her visit to Cambridge in a letter to a friend. She was writing in the early 19thC but there can be few visitors to the city today who don't share her wonder at the architectural splendour of the historic colleges of Cambridge University.

The oldest college is Peterhouse, founded in 1284 by the Bishop of Ely. Clare was founded over a hundred years later, in 1338, and Pembroke was next in 1347. There are now 31 colleges and the latest is Robinson College, founded in 1974 by a local millionaire, but it's the early colleges with their mixture of architectural styles that are the most interesting to the visitor. Sited around the city centre, they're all within walking distance and although they're essentially private places where people live and work, if you are quiet and respect their privacy, you're welcome to stroll through the magnificent courtyards, look around the chapels and, in some cases, the halls and libraries. You don't actually need to know any dates or facts to appreciate the beauty of the buildings, but if you do want to find out more about the fascinating history of Cambridge and its colleges, then you can join one of the walking tours which leave regularly from the tourist information centre. The tours, which take two hours, vary depending on the size of group (large parties are not allowed in certain colleges) and activities within the colleges. However, you can expect to see a selection of the following: Corpus Christi, St Catharine's, Trinity, Pembroke, Downing, Emmanuel, Christ's and King's. You'll also hear about some of the famous characters who studied here including Lord Tennyson, Lord Byron, Sir Isaac Newton, Edward VII and more recently Prince Charles and his brother, Prince Edward.

Of all the colleges, King's is probably the most famous. Founded in 1441 by the young King Henry VI, it's the chapel that has always been the real centrepiece. You may have seen the interior on television – the glorious sound of King's College Choir singing seasonal carols and lessons has now become a Christmas tradition. But it's a completely different and very moving experience to see it with your own eyes. The Gothic-style fan-vaulted ceiling is arguably the most striking feature but other outstanding treasures in-

King's College Chapel

clude the 16thC stained-glass windows which tell the
story of the New Testament, and Rubens' great painting *The Adoration of the Magi* which dominates the
altar. If you have time while visiting the college, you
should try to see the exhibition on the building of
King's Chapel.

For the best view of the exterior of King's College
Chapel, walk through the college courtyard to the
banks of the River Cam. Around you is the area known
as the 'backs', a carpet of crocuses and daffodils in the
spring, the scene of many a picnic and punting party in
the summer, and a secluded and picturesque mixture
of lawns, formal gardens, open spaces and bridges at
any time of year. A leisurely walk along the 'backs' is
the perfect way to end your visit and reflect on the
history of Cambridge and its colleges.

Practical details

Tourist Information Centre, Wheeler St. (0223) 322640.
Open Apr–Oct 09.00 (09.30 Wed)–18.00 Mon–Fri,
09.00–17.00 Sat; Easter & May–Sep 10.30–15.30 Sun &
Bank Hols; Nov–Mar 09.00–17.30 Mon–Fri,
09.00–17.00 Sat.

Walking Tours (visiting the major colleges as available including King's College Chapel if possible). Apr–Jun 11.00 & 14.00 Mon–Sat; mid Jun–mid Sep 11.00, 13.00, 14.00 & 15.00 Mon–Sat; mid Sep–mid Oct 11.00, 13.00 & 14.00 Mon–Sat; mid Oct–Nov 11.00 & 14.00 Mon–Sat; Dec–Mar 14.00 Sat; Apr–Sep 11.15 Sun & Bank Hols. Charge.
Historic City Tour Jul–Aug 18.30 Tue, Wed, Fri–Sun. Charge.
Drama Tour Jul–Aug 18.30 Mon & Thur. Charge.

King's College Chapel Exhibition Open mid Mar–mid Oct 09.30–15.30 (17.00 in vacations except second half of Jul) Mon–Sat, 11.00–17.00 Sun (in vacations only); mid Oct–mid Mar 11.00–15.30 (17.00 in vacations) Mon–Sat; 12.00–15.30 Sun (in vacations only). Charge.
Rail Liverpool Street to Cambridge (1hr).
Coach National Express Victoria to Cambridge (1hr 50mins). Green Line Victoria to Cambridge (2hrs 30mins).
Nearby Audley End (12 miles), Ely (16 miles), Newmarket (14 miles), Wimpole Hall (14 miles).

TREAT!

If your tour of the colleges has whet your appetite for more knowledge about Cambridge then head for the Folk Museum, a fascinating Aladdin's Cave of exhibits ranging from children's toys to farm equipment which tell the story of the people who have lived in and around the city over the past few hundred years. There's also a room set aside for displays on the history of Cambridge and the University including the standard weights and measures used by the University to check that all trading was honest. As well as its permanent collections, the museum has changing exhibitions.

Folk Museum, 2/3 Castle St. (0223) 355159. Open 10.30–17.00 Mon–Sat & 14.30–16.30 Sun. Charge.

TREAT!

CANTERBURY
55 miles E

Canterbury Heritage, a 'time-walk' museum, should
be where you start your trip if you are a first-time visitor to Canterbury. Housed in the attractive, medieval,
Poor Priest's Hospital building, the museum imaginatively presents – using holograms, computer displays,
pilgrim souvenirs, Civil War armour and a Stephenson
railway engine – the city's long and fascinating history.

In AD602 St Augustine was given the original
church where Canterbury Cathedral now stands.
Today's magnificent building, the focal point for
world-wide Anglicanism, annually draws thousands of
tourists. The cathedral possesses a wonderful sense of
space, with differing architectural periods and styles
juxtaposed on varying levels, all lit by dramatic natural
light which streams in through the mainly unstained
windows. The picturesque surrounding close and precincts contain the tomb of Edward the Black Prince
and the royal monument of Henry IV and his queen,
Joan of Navarre. You can also wander through Green
Court which is surrounded by the buildings of King's
School, England's oldest public school where the
pupils still wear winged collars and boaters. In one
corner of Green Court you can see a fine Norman
staircase and nearby a Norman gateway.

Other interesting remains in the city include a
Roman mosaic pavement and hypocaust room. Unfortunately, the underground museum in which the
remains, along with other archaeological finds, are
housed is rather dusty and uninspiring, but the exhibits
themselves are well worth a look. More immediately
attractive is West Gate, the city's only surviving for-
tified gatehouse. Dating from 1380 it was used as a
prison for a long period and you may visit the cells in
the tower. Another historic building, but much less
well known (perhaps because it is both hard to find and
rarely open), is Greyfriars. Tucked away down an

unprepossessing back street and reached by crossing a small foot-bridge over the River Stour, Greyfriars is a charming 13thC house which once belonged to the first Franciscans to settle in England. Today only four rooms survive. Of those, the main upper room is now a chapel while in the lower rear room you can see a small trap door which is thought to have been constructed to allow the monks to fish from the river which flows beneath.

Most of Canterbury's other attractions are easier to find – like Eastbridge Hospital on the main street. Behind its façade, part medieval flint and part 17thC brick, you can visit a little Chantry Chapel and a 12thC vaulted undercroft which was used as a dormitory for pilgrims who bedded down for the night on its rush-strewn floor. A flight of stairs leads to an elegant late-12thC refectory which still has its original wall paintings showing Christ in Glory.

Wandering from attraction to attraction in Canterbury you are not only exploring this fine medieval city, but following in the footsteps of many a pilgrim. As Geoffrey Chaucer, one of the city's most famous observers, wrote in *The Canterbury Tales*, 'from every shire's end of England to Canterbury they wend'.

Practical details

Tourist Information Centre, 13 Longmarket. (0227) 766567.

Leisureline 24hr telephone service gives details of events. (0227) 67744.
Canterbury Cathedral open 07.15–19.00 (to 18.30 Oct–Mar) Mon–Sun. Free.
Canterbury Heritage, Poor Priest's Hospital, Stour St. (0227) 452747. Open 10.30–16.00 Mon–Sat. Charge.
Eastbridge Hospital of St Thomas of Canterbury,

High St. Open Mon–Sun but times vary. Donation.
Greyfriars, off Stour St. Open Jun–Sep but times vary (see notice on door). Donation.
Roman Pavement, Butchery Lane. (0227) 452747. Open 10.00–13.00 & 14.00–17.00 (to 16.00 Oct–Mar) Mon–Sat. Charge.
West Gate, St Dunstan's St. (0227) 452747. Open as

for Roman Pavement.
Charge.
Rail Victoria to
Canterbury (1hr).

Coach National Express
Victoria to Canterbury
(1hr 45mins).
Nearby Leeds Castle (16
miles).

TREAT!

Take a short excursion by train (10 minutes) to the small seaside town of Whitstable, once the port of Canterbury. Despite its fame for being the last stop on the line of the world's first passenger railway, Whitstable has lost none of its seafaring heritage. It has retained its working harbour along with its reputation for delicious oysters! You could arrange your visit to coincide with the Oyster Festival in July. For details of this, and other events, contact the Tourist Information Centre, Horsebridge, High St, Whitstable. (0227) 275482.

TREAT!

CHESSINGTON WORLD OF ADVENTURES
15 miles SW

There aren't any 'white knuckle' rides at Chessington; the aim is to excite and delight rather than scare claim the organisers. But you still need nerves of steel and a pretty strong stomach to stay smiling through *all* the thrills and spills. It's very busy, very colourful and highly commercial but once there you can't help but get caught up in the carnival atmosphere. Chessington has been designed to give the whole family a great day out – and it certainly succeeds. If you can survive the hustle of the crowds, then there is something for all ages to enjoy and the entrance charge covers everything so you can have as many rides as you can fit into the day.

Chessington World of Adventures really is a theme park with the various 'worlds' occupying separate areas and all distinctly different. The 'Mystic East' is dominated by a huge Japanese Buddha looking down on the eastern 'world' of dainty fans and spicy delicacies with its elegant palace, eastern market, oriental-style landscape and the amazing water ride on Dragon River. The ride splashes its way up and down, up and down the dramatic dips, and ends with an exhilarating surprise. At the other side of the globe is the western 'world' where you can try your skills at Rick O'Shea's Shooting Gallery or grab a bite to eat at Miners Diner. But you need the courage of a cowboy to risk the trip on the Runaway Mine Train. Fast and furious, it careers through dark and dangerous territory in 'Calamity Canyon' where you can experience the 'Californian Goldrush'. Another whole new 'world' can be found at 'Fifth Dimension', the land of fantasy which is captured on a giant computer screen.

Small children and less adventurous adults may prefer the quieter charms of the 'Market Square', which is a re-creation of an English village with a Norman castle, a mill wheel, a pond and, of course, the village pub. The rides here are equally gentle with the Old Crocks Rally, and the Chessington Railroad which takes you round the park giving a good overall view. Another corner especially for younger members of the family is the lively 'Circus World'. Here a professional team of acrobats, trapeze artists and jugglers stage energetic shows in an area surrounded by play equipment for little ones to test their own circus expertise. And who can resist a ride on the Flying Jumbo? These pink elephants aren't the only animals at Chessington, which was a zoo long before it was a theme park, and creatures great and small still live in and around the different 'worlds'. A Safari Skyway monorail takes visitors high above the animals while the familiar voice of Johnny Morris talks you through them all. Exhausted? Now you see why you're advised to come early and stay late; you need at least four or five hours to get your money's worth.

Practical details

Chessington World of Adventures, Leatherhead Rd, Chessington, Surrey. (03727) 27227.

Open all attractions Apr–Oct 10.00–17.00 Mon–Sun. Zoo open all year 10.00–16.00 Mon–Sun. Closed Christmas Day.
Admission charge.
Disabled facilities good but avoid busy times (weekends & school hols).
Other facilities free car park, toilets, mother and baby room, refreshment facilities, picnic areas and tent, gift shops. No dogs allowed.
Rail Waterloo or Clapham Junction to Chessington South (30mins) followed by 10min walk.
Coach Green Line Victoria direct (40mins).
Nearby Thorpe Park (8 miles), Windsor (16 miles), Wisley (12 miles).

TREAT!

If you've been too busy on the rides to taste any of the variety of victuals available at Chessington, when you leave head for The Star – a friendly pub which caters for big appetites. Hot and cold food is available and you can be sure of a plate loaded with good wholesome cooking. Children are welcome in the large garden.

The Star, Leatherhead Rd. (0372) 842416.

TREAT!

COTSWOLD WILD LIFE PARK
75 miles W

The 180 acres (72.9ha) of gardens and woodland in which the Cotswold Wild Life Park is set ensures that visitors rarely feel crowded even on a popular summer weekend. There are grassland areas, a walled garden and a wide variety of animal enclosures. One particu-

Rhinos, Cotswold Wild Life Park

larly enjoyable aspect of the park is the opportunity to see a variety of animals roaming in relative freedom. To a large extent it is the public rather than the wild life which is restricted and visitors must keep to carefully controlled walks guarded by ditches and fences. The animals, including zebras, rhinos, deer, wallabies, antelope, and even red pandas may choose to come and 'inspect' their visitors when, and if, they wish. However, some of the more dangerous species, like the leopards, are kept firmly caged.

Children, especially, seem to appreciate the park and there's plenty for them to do with a popular adventure playground and a children's farmyard where tame animals – pigs, lambs, goats, llamas, ducks, rabbits – can be stroked. When the weather's good there are pony rides, but the main family attraction is the narrow gauge railway which operates in the park during the summer months. There is an additional charge for some of these amenities.

Collections of birds, monkeys and reptiles can also be seen, while in the tropical house there are many exotic plants. Living amongst the foliage you may spot small tropical birds including the eyecatching iridescent humming bird.

Most popular of all the park's attractions, however, is the penguin pool. Get a good position at feeding time

(11.00 and 16.00 every day except Friday) to see these appealing creatures at their most active.

During the summer a host of extra attractions are laid on including 'snake days'. Many people are frightened of snakes, or think them slimy and unpleasant, while some people even believe that they can sting with their tongues. At a snake day these myths are exploded as the visitors are given the chance to examine snakes at close quarters and discuss them with knowledgeable staff who are on hand to answer any questions. Other special events include morris dancing, car rallies, a donkey show and a falconry flying display.

Practical details

Cotswold Wild Life Park, Burford, Oxon. (099 382) 3006.

Open 10.00–18.00 (or dusk) every day except Christmas Day.
Admission charge.
Disabled facilities good, invalid chairs (free) available on request.
Other facilities parking, restaurant, bars, refreshment kiosks, gift shops, first aid post, brass rubbing centre (telephone for opening times).
No public transport
Nearby Blenheim Palace (18 miles), Oxford (20 miles).

TREAT!

A few miles down the road can be found Cotswold Woollen Weavers. This active mill has a small museum which contains examples of handlooms, stitching machines and an evocative selection of early photographs. You can buy some Cotswold weaving, made on the premises. This material has been highly prized over the years and 12thC weavers used to sing 'in Europe the best wool's English, in England the best wool's Cotswold'.

Cotswold Woollen Weavers, Filkins, Glos. (036786) 491. Open 10.00–18.00 Mon–Sat, 14.00–18.00 Sun.

TREAT!

DRUSILLAS
55 miles SE

Can you bend down and touch the ground five times while standing on one leg without falling over? This is what young visitors to Drusillas are invited to do in an attempt to copy a flamingo who can stand on one leg for hours and feed at the same time. Most try, but many, much to their own and everyone else's amusement, find they simply can't compete with the flamingo at the balancing act. This challenge is part of the popular 'Zoolympics', a series of animal antics, involving both mental and physical exercises, designed with an imaginative blend of humour and educational value to help introduce children to the world of animals and birds.

Drusillas began life as a pets' corner at a tea shop back in the 1920s and is still run by the same family. Friendly and informal, if a little chaotic at times, it's small, covering some 20 acres (8.1ha) in all, and aimed especially at small people. To ensure no one is frightened, the 400 or so inhabitants are all small too. Indeed, the largest animal is probably the llama. The park is laid out in themed areas including the 'Australian Outback' with wallabies, emus and Cape Barren geese; the award-winning 'Beaver Country'; the Butterfly House and the Farmyard. Special care has been taken to ensure there's easy access throughout for prams and wheelchairs, and doors and windows are placed at just the right height for inquisitive eyes to watch and tiny hands to touch.

The main thrust of Drusillas is on education, with the emphasis on doing rather than viewing and learning through activity. Work sheets and school packs are available and a double-decker bus has been converted to provide 'hands-on' experience. You can, for example, actually feel the weight of an elephant's tooth or measure the length of a giant python. This is very much a place for children. They can be seen everywhere – scribbling notes on quiz sheets, sketching, taking part in the 'Zoolympics' or riding on the train pulled by two engines, Emily and Bill. The children's squeals of delight can be heard just about everywhere, too. Drusillas offers an ideal introduction to different animals although older children may not find it exciting enough to be so stimulating and for anyone without children, it can all get rather frenetic.

Some peace and quiet can be found in the formal Japanese and Rose Gardens which have plenty of strategically placed seats so weary adults can catch their breath. Next to the gardens is the village with different craft shops and a small garden centre. And if you're feeling hungry, it's well worth sampling a cream tea or snack in the Thatched Barn while the children complete their day out with a special 'kiddies cocktail'.

Practical details

Drusillas, Alfriston, East Sussex. (0323) 870234.

Open all year 10.30–17.00 (last admission) Mon–Sun. Closed Christmas Day and Boxing Day. Some attractions closed Nov–Mar. Phone for details.
Admission charge.
Disabled facilities access.
Other facilities free car park, toilets, pocket money shops, café, pub/restaurant and picnic area, bakery and wine centre, special events.

Rail Victoria to Berwick (1hr 30mins) and then taxi (or walk). Victoria to Eastbourne (1hr 40mins) and then bus (summer only).
Coach National Express Victoria to Eastbourne (2hrs 30mins) and then bus (summer only).
Nearby Battle Abbey (16 miles), Bluebell Railway (14 miles), Brighton (15 miles).

TREAT!

Save some time to visit historic Alfriston with its medieval timber-framed houses. Near to the old market cross is the Smuggling Inn, a reminder of the village's infamous past. The friendly pub, a maze of doors, rooms and staircases was once the

home and hideout of local smuggler and butcher
Stanton Collins and now makes a novel venue for a
bar snack. There is a beer garden at the back.

The Smuggling Inn, Market Cross. (0323) 870241.
_____ *TREAT!*

ELY CATHEDRAL
78 miles N

Rising high above the flat Fens landscape, Ely Cathedral dominates the skyline for miles around. Massive
and magnificent, it draws people like a magnet. Ely has
long been a home of prayer and its religious base dates
back to the 7thC when Queen Ethelreda founded an
abbey for both monks and nuns here on her estates. It's
interesting to note that the administrative area of Ely
at that time was an island, known as the Isle of Eels,
and stayed until the Fens were drained in the 17th
and 18thC. Explanations for its original name are
fascinating. One version says that it derives from the
diet of the Saxons who lived there, but the more
popular story is that St Dunstan was so offended by the
'married' state of monks living in the abbey that he
turned them all into eels.

The present cathedral, the third on the site, was built
in 1081 and completed by the Normans in around 1200.
Widely recognised as an outstanding example of
medieval architecture, it boasts many fine features: the
rich carvings in the Prior's Door; the beautifully decorated 14thC Lady's Chapel; and the Victorian painted
ceilings, the work of two amateurs. But it's the incredible Octagon that is the real inspiration. This
eight-sided lantern was the masterpiece of Alan of
Walsingham and is a unique replacement for the central tower which collapsed in 1322. All eyes look
upward at this superb feat of engineering and minds

Ely Cathedral

marvel at the ornate mass of lead, timber and glass weighing some 400 tons, which appears to hang without support, suspended in mid-air. The cathedral is a fitting setting for the Stained Glass Museum, to be found high up in the North Triforium overlooking the long nave. This national collection of ecclesiastical and domestic stained glass has been rescued from redundant churches and other buildings. Well-lit and positioned at eye-level, it's a rare opportunity to study the fine craftsmanship at close quarters. Displays in the museum also describe the history of stained glass and show how techniques and styles have changed over the years.

The cathedral precincts are rich in historic monastic buildings, many of which are now part of King's School, the successor to the school where Edward the Confessor is said to have been educated. Of special note are the Ely Porta which is the original three-storey gatehouse to the Benedictine Priory built in 1397; and Prior Crauden's Chapel with its mosaic tile pavement and 19thC stained glass. To find out the full background of the cathedral and city of Ely, so rich in character, history and fascinating stories, it's worth joining a guided tour (tickets available from the Tourist Information Centre on the day). The tours last 1½ hours and tell you all the essential information, so you can enjoy the splendid architecture and charming surroundings at your leisure. If time allows, do wander through the park which leads down to the River Ouse, offering walks and quiet picnic spots.

Practical details

Ely Cathedral, Ely, Cambs. (0353) 667735/6 (the Chapter House).

Open Apr–Sep 07.00–19.00 Mon–Sun; Oct–Mar 07.30–18.00 Mon–Sat (to 17.00 Sun). *Admission* donation. *Disabled facilities* limited. *Other facilities* toilets nearby, gift shop, refectory serving meals and snacks, tours of the West Tower, Brass Rubbing Centre (open Easter–Jun Sat & Sun; Jul & Aug Mon–Sun. For times check noticeboard. Charge). *Guided tours* Jun–Aug 14.30 Thur, 11.00 Sat (Jul & Aug only). Charge. Tickets from Tourist Information Centre, the Library, Palace Green. (0354) 662062. *Stained Glass Museum*, North Triforium, Ely Cathedral. (0353) 5103. Open Mar–Oct 11.00–16.00 Mon–Fri, 11.00–16.30 Sat & Bank Hols, 12.00–15.00 Sun. Charge. *Rail* Liverpool Street to Ely (1hr 25mins). *Coach* National Express Victoria to Ely (2hrs 5mins). *Nearby* Cambridge (16 miles), Grafham Water (25 miles), Newmarket (12 miles).

TREAT!

Tucked away down a narrow lane leading from the A142 just a few miles from Ely is Shades Mill at Soham. The old smock mill (a type of windmill), dates back to the 18thC but has now been renovated, and makes an unusual place to stop for some refreshment. Homely snacks are served in the adjoining house.

Shades Mill, 12 The Shade, Soham. (0353) 720859. Open 10.30–17.30 Sat, Sun & Bank Hols.

TREAT!

GOODWOOD RACES
60 miles SW

'A garden party with racing tacked on' was Edward VII's fond description of a day at Goodwood Races earlier this century. The same holds true today; the convivial atmosphere, the beautiful setting high on the South Downs and the top-quality racing make 'Glorious Goodwood' one of the best introductions to horseracing and a pleasurable day for both expert and amateur.

Races are held at Goodwood on set days from May to September. The July five-day festival is internationally famous and enormously popular. For a less crowded day out, choose a May meeting when the course looks brilliantly green with the beeches bursting into new life. Newcomers are often put off by worries about racing jargon and etiquette, but it's surprising how quickly you can pick up what's going on. And the more you begin to understand about racing, the more you'll enjoy the day so don't just sit on the sidelines – wander around, keeping your eyes and ears open. Dress is informal yet smart; gone are the days of top hat and tails but jeans and t-shirts won't be appreciated. Comfortable shoes are essential as there's a lot of standing and walking involved; and you're well-advised to wrap up warmly as it can get rather blowy.

Much of the car parking is free but you pay to get into the race-course, the amount depending on where you choose to watch the racing. The Richmond Enclosure is the most exclusive spot, overlooking the winning post. However, you can also get a good view of the course from the Grandstand and the Public Enclosures. Once inside, your first step should be to buy a racecard which lists the races of the day, the horses expected to run and the official form. You'll find a full explanation of all the abbreviations and racing 'shorthand' in the racecard; within minutes you know all about the breeding of each horse, his previous performance, weight, age, jockey, trainer and other information intended to help you make an informed selection.

Now find your way to the Paddock which is a hub of activity between races. This is where the horses parade before the next race; and afterwards where the winning owner is presented with the trophy. As the horses are walked around, this is your chance to look at them closely before making your final decision and placing your bet. Time, too, to enjoy the view across Paddock Lawn, over the spire of Chichester Cathedral and, on a clear day, to the Isle of Wight beyond. Most newcomers opt to bet with the Tote, but if you fancy trying to 'beat the book', take a look at the advice in the racecard on betting with the bookmakers. It certainly adds that extra excitement to the day.

As the horses are ridden to the start, spectators jostle for position and the tension starts to rise. Silence falls as they set off at a fast and furious pace, everyone either alert to the commentary or peering hopefully through binoculars. Then come the loud and encouraging cheers, the tears and the triumph as fortunes, large and small, are made and lost. You've won? Well, wait for the call, collect your winnings and splash out on champagne or a cream tea – there are certainly no shortage of places to celebrate at Goodwood.

Practical details

Goodwood Racecourse, Goodwood, Chichester, West Sussex. (0243) 774107.

Open May–Sep selected days and evenings.
Admission charge.
Disabled facilities good access.
Other facilities free car parks, toilets, gift shop, café, bars and restaurant, picnic areas (including 3 Furlong Picnic Park for cars), children's playground, binocular hire.
Rail Victoria to Chichester (1hr 40mins) then race-day coach to the course.
Coach National Express Victoria to Chichester (3hrs 10mins) then race-day coach to the course.

Nearby Butlin's Southcoast World (8 miles), Portsmouth (20 miles), Weald and Downland Open Air Museum (6 miles).

TREAT!

For a slap-up meal before or after the racing, try the nearby Goodwood Park Hotel. Newly refurbished and extended, it may at first appear a surprising venue for an intimate meal. But the hotel's Dukes' Restaurant is tastefully decorated and offers a magnificent selection of light, French-style foods. If time is short, you can grab a snack in the Richmond Arms bar.

Goodwood Park Hotel, Goodwood. (0243) 775537.

TREAT!

GRAFHAM WATER
60 miles N

It's really only from the air that you can get a true picture of the full extent of Grafham Water, one of the largest man-made lakes in the country. But to give some indication of its size, this vast reservoir covers a surface area of 2½ square miles and contains some 13,000 million gallons of water. It's essentially a bulk water supply project serving nearly 1½ million people in the neighbouring five counties, but it now has so much on offer with sailing, fishing, a nature reserve, bird-observation hides, picnic spots and scenic walks that it's fast becoming a major tourist attraction.

The shoreline of Grafham Water covers around 9 miles (15km) and you can walk much of it, with the exclusion of the 370-acre (149.9ha) Nature Reserve at the western end. There are three public car parks, each providing picnic spots, refreshments and starting points for rambles. Don't worry if the car park looks full because within minutes of leaving your car, everyone else seems to disappear and you feel as though you have the whole place to yourself. Perhaps one of the prettiest places to park is just west of the village of Perry, in Mander Park. This is both the start of the Nature Reserve and home of the Fishing Lodge. The trout in the reservoir are particularly plump with fishermen boasting record catches. Fishing permits can be bought from the lodge and tackle and boats are available for hire. Mander Park is also a favourite spot for feeding ducks, especially in the winter when the reservoir is noted for its plentiful number and variety. Indeed, Grafham's ducks have now become such an institution locally that notices warn motorists to slow down for ducks crossing the road – usually, it seems, to get to the local pub!

To find out more about the story behind the reservoir, which was officially opened in 1966, it's well worth calling into the Residential Centre (which runs an excellent selection of weekend courses if you're interested). You can pick up a free guide here to the water's wildlife giving some suggested walks from the centre, and next door is the busy Grafham Water Sailing Club where non-members can sail or sailboard at a daily rate. Standards are impressive, and there are some stunning performances to be watched in the high winds.

Practical details

Grafham Water, Perry, Huntingdon, Cambs.

Open all the time.
Admission free.
Disabled facilities very good access.
Other facilities free car parks, toilets, refreshment kiosks, nature trails.
Further details of facilities from Anglian Water, Cambridge Division,
Great Ouse House, Clarendon Rd, Cambridge. (0223) 61561.
Beds and Hunts Wildlife Trust, Priory Country Park, Barkers Lane, Bedford. (0234) 64213.
Grafham Water Trout Fishery. (0480) 810531.
Open Apr–Oct

08.00–22.00 (or dusk)
Mon–Sun.
*Grafham Water
Residential Centre.* (0480)
810521. Open 09.00–17.00
Mon–Sun.
*Grafham Water Sailing
Club.* (0480) 810521.
Open 09.00–20.00
Wed–Sun.
Rail King's Cross to
Huntingdon (1hr) and
then taxi. King's Cross to
St Neots (40mins) and
then taxi.
Coach Whippet Coaches
King's Cross to Buckden
and then taxi.
Nearby Cambridge (25
miles), Ely (25 miles),
Shuttleworth Collection
(16 miles), Wimpole Hall
(28 miles).

TREAT!

Follow those ducks to the pub – they know where
you can get a good pint. The Wheatsheaf at West
Perry is a favourite watering hole for Grafham's
sailors and fishermen whose tales get taller as their
glasses get emptier. Cosy in the winter and with a
spacious garden for sunny days, home-cooked
food is available seven days a week.

The Wheatsheaf, West Perry. (0480) 810253.

TREAT!

GREAT DIXTER HOUSE AND
GARDENS
52 miles SE

Nowhere could provide a greater contrast to London
than the house and gardens at Great Dixter. Well off
the beaten track and seemingly hidden within a web of
country lanes, it is a haven of peace, tranquillity and
beauty. Though relatively small, in comparison to
many country houses and estates, Great Dixter has
plenty to encourage you to linger.

The manor of Dixter dates back to 1220, but most of
the timber-framed building seen today is 15th and

16thC. Its evolution this century has, however, been unusual. The original 15thC front section of Great Dixter was bought in 1910 by Nathaniel Lloyd who entrusted its restoration and enlargement to architect Sir Edwin Lutyens (1869–1944). Architect and client then made a bold move – they extended the manor by attaching a 16thC yeoman's hall-house. This additional timbered property was bought in a derelict state for £75 then dismantled, restored, and rebuilt, behind the original manor. Lutyens further extended Great Dixter with the design of new domestic accommodation which stretches from the entrance porch out to the left. The house is still inhabited by members of the Lloyd family, so only part of the interior can be viewed, but you can see enough to gain a good impression of the clever merger of styles and periods.

As you enter the hall, try to imagine how it would have looked originally – with an earth floor and a central open hearth. Then look up and you will notice that there are two types of roof construction: tie beams with king posts above, and six hammer beams – it is a combination which is thought to be unique. While looking up, also note the circular light fittings which were designed by Lutyens and based on the shape of children's toy hoops! You can see a portrait of this influential architect at the bottom of the staircase which leads to the solar (the withdrawing room of the lord of the manor).

Out in the garden the work of Lutyens is once again in evidence. The overall impression created by the garden is of a series of rooms, each with an individual character. There are high hedges, meandering path-ways, deceptive brick walls and, best of all, delightful wild areas filled with daffodils, grasses and a host of meadow flowers. Many of the original farmyard build-ings were incorporated into the design of the garden including a three-kiln oasthouse, last used for drying hops in 1939. The sunken garden with octagonal pool, in front of the oasthouse, was created to the design of Nathaniel Lloyd (encouraged by Lutyens) who eventually became a practising architect himself.

Practical details

Great Dixter House and Gardens, Northiam, East Sussex. (07974) 3160.

Open Apr–mid Oct 14.00–17.00 (last admission) Tue–Sun & Bank Hol Mons.
Admission charge.
Disabled access unsuitable for wheelchairs.
Other facilities special guided tours by prior arrangement, free car park, plants on sale, picnic area.
No public transport
Nearby Battle (8 miles), Rye and Winchelsea (8 miles), Whitbread Hop Farm (20 miles).

TREAT!

Bodiam, an extraordinarily picturesque medieval castle, is only a few miles away, down winding country lanes. Its interior is ruined, but the exterior makes it a very special place to visit. Completely moated, its turreted walls seem to float on what appears (on a clear, sunny day) to be a shimmering mirror, while all around spread the green flood plains of the River Rother.

Bodiam Castle, Robertsbridge. (058083) 436.

Bodiam Castle

TREAT!

HATFIELD HOUSE
25 miles N

A fine Jacobean house (built 1607–11); a surviving wing from the Royal Palace of Hatfield (1497); fine gardens and an encompassing Great Park all combine to make Hatfield a beautiful place to visit. It is also a place of historical significance. Here Henry VIII's younger daughter, Elizabeth, spent most of her youth (virtually a prisoner during the reign of her sister Mary) and here she heard the news of Mary's death and therefore her accession. The young queen's first Council of State (November 1558) was held in the hall of the Royal Palace of Hatfield and she appointed William Cecil (1520–1598) to be her Chief Minister. You can see two famous portraits of Elizabeth in the present house. The *Ermine Portrait* by Nicholas Hilliard – court painter, miniaturist and goldsmith – takes its name from the image of an ermine positioned on her sleeve; a symbol of the queen's purity and virginity. The *Rainbow Portrait* (attributed to Isaac Oliver c1565–1617) is also symbolic. Elizabeth's dress is covered with an unusual decorative motif of eyes and ears which suggests that the wearer could see and hear everything which happened in her kingdom. The serpent on her sleeve is the emblem of wisdom and the rainbow in her hand is the symbol of peace.

While wandering around the house look carefully at the decorative detailing – there are clues to all sorts of stories. Look, for example, at the pretty carving of a man with a rake on the newel at the top of the fine, cantilevered, grand staircase: he's thought to be John Tradescant (d1637), gardener and adventurer, who travelled extensively to hitherto unknown parts of the world in search of exotic plants. Incidentally, the carved gates at the foot of the stairs were to stop dogs running about on the upper floors. More intimate items to look out for include Queen Elizabeth I's hat, gloves and stockings – the silk stockings are believed to be the first pair worn in England. In the library, which contains a collection of around 10,000 books dating from the mid 16thC, you can see letters written by Mary Queen of Scots along with Lord Burghley's (William Cecil's) rough draft of the warrant ordering her execution.

Practical details

Hatfield House, Hatfield, Herts. (07072) 62823.

Open mid Mar–mid Sep 12.00–17.00 Tue–Fri, 14.00–17.30 Sun & 11.00–17.00 Bank Hol Mons. Closed Good Fri & over Christmas
Admission charge (visits to house by guided tour only, except Sun).
Disabled facilities access limited.
Other facilities shop, restaurant, toilets, garden shop, medieval banquets, car park, open space for picnicking. No dogs allowed.

Rail King's Cross to Hatfield (20 mins). Combined rail travel/admission tickets available.
Coach Green Line from Victoria to Hatfield (1hr).
Nearby Knebworth (12 miles), St Albans (5 miles).

⌐ *TREAT!*

If you fancy following in the footsteps of Charles Dickens, have a pint at the 'olde-worlde' Eight Bells on the corner of Fore Street. Dickens stayed here and one of his fictional characters, Bill Sikes (in *Oliver Twist*), took refuge here after murdering Nancy.

The Eight Bells, 2 Park St. (07072) 66059.

TREAT! ⌐

THE HAWK CONSERVANCY
80 miles SW

Minutes away from a busy dual carriageway, the Hawk
Conservancy is a surprisingly restful spot. The birds,
which are kept in cages or tethered to stumps, are
confined to a relatively small area through which the
public is free to wander. As its name suggests, the
Hawk Conservancy is a specialist bird of prey centre.
You can see a wide variety of species including hawks,
owls, falcons, eagles, vultures and kites. While you are
wandering around the conservancy you may be struck
by how lifeless the birds seem. Vultures sit hunched on
a branch, eagles rarely seem to move, and owls of all
sizes look like bundles of feathers only momentarily
showing a sign of life by briefly opening a large eye. Yet
these still, silent creatures are transformed when it is
their turn to fly.

Flying demonstrations are given every afternoon
and are the real highlights of a visit to the conservancy,
but try and go on a fine day as the birds are not flown
during very wet or windy weather. Different species
are flown completely free at each demonstration
providing a good opportunity to photograph them
swooping and gliding: you may even be allowed to hold
one of them. The conservancy is probably the only
place in England which demonstrates some of the
spectacular movements of the peregrine falcon. It is
also the only place to watch a group of some six or
seven black kites being flown together. The first
demonstration of the day (12.00) is designed with
children and school parties in mind. This means that
birds children are more likely to see – such as buzzards,
barn owls and kestrels – are displayed, and the explanation of techniques and the history of falconry is
simplified. The later demonstrations are for adults and
involve more unusual birds of prey such as the golden
eagle. Each demonstration lasts a minimum of 30

minutes, and it's well worth stopping to watch two or three flights, perhaps having a picnic lunch or a cup of tea in between.

Practical details

Hawk Conservancy, Weyhill, Nr Andover, Hants. (026 477) 2252.

Open Mar–Oct
10.30–16.00 Mon–Sun.
Flying demonstrations
12.00, 14.00, 15.00, 16.00
Mon–Sun.
Admission charge.
Disabled facilities access.

Other facilities toilets (but not for the disabled), shop, picnic tables, café, photography allowed.
No public transport
Nearby Avebury (22 miles), Salisbury (16 miles), Winchester (16 miles).

TREAT!

Birds of prey have been flown by humans for many centuries, but in the vicinity of the conservancy you can visit the remains of several Iron Age settlements where the idea of using them as hunters was probably unknown. First pay a visit to Andover Museum where displays outline community life during the Iron Age and its subsequent overthrow by the Romans some 2000 years ago. Then take a look at Danebury Hill Fort which claims to be Europe's most studied Iron Age hill settlement. It is thought that Danebury was once one of southern England's very first trading towns, but today it is only a well-excavated hilltop surrounded by beautiful woodland.

Andover Museum, 6 Church Close. (0264) 66283. Open 10.00–17.00 Tue–Sat. Charge for Iron Age Experience.
Danebury Hill Fort (5 miles SW of Andover). (0962) 64221. Open all the time. Free.

TREAT!

HEVER CASTLE AND GARDENS
30 miles S

Hever Castle is known today as the romantic setting for
Anne Boleyn's courtship by King Henry VIII. Its
compact fortress-like exterior – with massive 13thC
gatehouse, arrow slits, turrets, water-filled moat and
portcullis drawbridge – belie the 15thC manor house to
be found inside. The comfortable Tudor accommodation, within the protective walls, dates from the
ill-fated Bullen family's occupation. For the visitor, the
first surprise is the remarkably domestic courtyard just
beyond the portcullis. Once inside, the atmosphere is
of a home rather than a castle. The Inner Hall is
decorated with lavishly carved Italian walnut dating
from 1905 and is home to portraits of Henry VIII (by
Holbein), Anne Boleyn and her sister Mary (in the
manner of Holbein), and Edward VI (by Scrots). You
can also see the Long Gallery, housing a reconstruction of a royal visit to Hever, and the splendid Dining
Hall, which in the Bullen's time was the Great Hall.
However, don't be deceived: the elegant linenfold
panelling, the carved minstrel gallery and the Bullen
arms are not Tudor – they are part of the reconstruction of the castle which took place between 1903 and
1906. Bought by an American, William Waldorf
Astor, millions of dollars were then lavished upon
Hever. Not only was it restored and refurbished, it was
also extended. The incongruous, but picturesque,
Tudor Village clustering behind the castle is part of this
20thC development, as are the gardens and lake.

In fact one of the real delights of a visit to Hever is
the opportunity to wander through its gardens, which
have been thoughtfully laid out to create interest all the
year round. In spring a yellow flood of daffodils seems
to burst through the grounds. Then, just a little later, a
haze of blossom – pear, apple and cherry – hovers over
budding azaleas and rhododendrons. In June the

walled rose garden is at its loveliest, while in autumn the tree-lined walks are the star attraction. The Italian Garden is fascinating all year round. This formal setting perfectly displays a large collection of classical statuary and sculpture including columns, urns, sarcophagi and statues, some of which are over 2000 years old. Running the whole length of the southern side of the Italian Garden, and providing a sharp contrast, is the Pergola Walk. Here, amongst moss-covered grottoes, thrive clematis, wisteria, honeysuckle, laburnum and camellias. Young visitors are also catered for: it really *is* possible to get lost in the mature maze – there is some quarter of a mile of pathways.

Practical details

Hever Castle and Gardens, Hever, Nr Edenbridge, Kent. (0732) 865224.

Open Apr–Oct 11.00 (12.00 castle)–17.00 Mon–Sun.
Admission charge.
Disabled facilities access to gardens only.
Other facilities free parking, toilets, café, adventure playground, small garden centre, lakeside theatre, gift shop.

Rail Victoria to Hever (1hr) then 1 mile walk (no taxi).
Coach Green Line Victoria to Hever (1hr 30mins), Invictaway Victoria to Hever Castle (1hr 30mins).
Nearby Knole (8 miles), Penshurst Vineyards (8 miles), Whitbread Hop Farm (16 miles).

TREAT!

Time seems to have stood still in nearby Chiddingstone, an attractive row of 16th and 17thC houses. Timbered façades, projecting upper storeys, mullions and casement windows all conjure up a time long since past. However, come opening time everything changes. The quiet village street is quickly lined by cars whose occupants have disappeared into the popular Castle Inn. On a fine day customers pour out into the pub's pretty garden, but if you stay inside there's plenty of atmosphere as The Castle has been a hostelry for over 250 years. It's also one of the most popular eating places in the area. If you fancy bar food you could sample half a dozen giant snails in champagne and garlic butter, followed by a smoked salmon salad, and finished off with a chocolate torte. But if this isn't quite gourmet enough and you really want to splash out, try the restaurant – this is the place where the locals come to celebrate.

The Castle Inn, Chiddingstone. (0892) 870247. Booking essential for restaurant.

TREAT!

HOBBS CROSS OPEN FARM
15 miles N

Fresh air, fresh milk and equally fresh smells – Hobbs Cross is very much a working farm! The idea is to show visitors, especially children, what happens to meat and milk before they arrive in their wrapper or bottle in the supermarket, and to impress on them exactly what's involved in the running of a commercial dairy and livestock farm. So put on your strong shoes and old clothes, and head for Hobbs Cross . . .

Like any farm, there's always a buzz of activity but milking time is by far the most popular with visitors. The farm has a dairy herd of 400 pedigree black and white British Friesians and you can watch them being milked in the parlour at around 13.30 each day. Forget any romantic notions of a maid and milking stool, this is high-tech stuff with machines taking the place of hard-working hands. The yields are quite incredible. Each cow is expected to give around 12,800 pints of milk a year, and at their peak about 80 pints a day. Hobbs Cross has its own processing dairy where milk is pasteurised and bottled. Information boards explain everything that goes into producing a 'farm fresh pinta'. It's a good starting point for school and home projects – and quite an education for adults too.

Other favourites are the pig house where the high-pitched squeaks of piglets intermingle with the sluggish grunts of sows. Here you'll find sows with their new-born litters, sometimes as many as 15 piglets to one mother. Nearby is the poultry house with its chick rearing unit, where newly hatched chicks are kept at a constant temperature of 95°F. Then there's Muffin and Queenie the two mules plus ponies, donkeys, goats, geese, rabbits, beef cattle and a small flock of sheep, often with lambs. And how could anyone forget Pannie? A huge six-year-old pedigree Friesian bull, Pannie is father to most of the calves on the farm. A notice asks you to treat him with respect – no wonder, he weighs nearly three quarters of a ton!

There are guided tours available for groups, but for most visitors the best way to enjoy the farm is to follow the yellow arrows which take you around the various units, all explained clearly by information plaques. The animals, with one obvious exception, are very friendly and used to children. They're happy to be fed too – so bring some fruit and vegetable peelings. But leave your dogs at home, they're strictly not welcome. After you've looked around the farm, do save some time to browse in the shop; it's full of fresh farm produce, plus vegetables and flowers from the market garden.

Practical details

Hobbs Cross Open Farm, Theydon Garnon, Epping, Essex. (037 881) 2882.

Open 10.30–16.30 Mon–Sun throughout the year, including Bank Hols. Closed Christmas Day.
Admission charge.
Disabled facilities good access except to milking parlour viewing gallery.
Other facilities free car park, toilets, gift shop, café and picnic area, guided tours by arrangement.
Rail London Underground (Central Line) to Theydon Bois (50mins) and then taxi or walk for 1½ miles.
Nearby Hatfield (20 miles), St Albans (25 miles).

┌─ *TREAT!*

While visiting Hobbs Cross you're right on the edge of the huge and wonderful 6000-acre (2430ha) Epping Forest, once part of a royal hunting ground. There are some lovely woodland trails through the forest and plenty of open spaces, picnic spots and parking places, so why not complete your visit with a country walk? If you'd like to find out more about Epping Forest, past and present, there are some interesting exhibits at the museum housed in Queen Elizabeth's Hunting Lodge, an old Tudor building at Chingford.

Epping Forest Museum, Queen Elizabeth's Hunting Lodge, Chingford. Open Wed–Sun and Bank Hols 14.00–18.00 (or dusk in winter). Charge.

TREAT! ─┘

HUGHENDEN MANOR
40 miles W

Hughenden is an example of a relatively plain Georgian building which has been Gothicised. A Victorian antiquary, John Norris, had arches somewhat incongruously inserted into the drawing room and had the dining room recess elaborately moulded – alterations which were very much in keeping with fashionable taste of that time. However, it was one of the most famous Victorians, Benjamin Disraeli (1804–1881), who most completely changed the appearance of Hughenden. In 1858 he employed W. G. Lacey to install Gothic plaster vaults in the hall and then the architect Edward Buckton Lamb was commissioned to embellish the exterior. The result was a new parapet with pinnacles, and the reordering of the windows which are easily identified by the red brick he used.

Disraeli and his wife also took a keen interest in Hughenden's substantial gardens and extensive park-

Hughenden Manor

land. Disraeli particularly loved the woods in autumn and noted one October how: 'the limes [are] all golden, the beeches ruddy brown, while the oaks and the elms and pines are still dark and green, and contrast well with the brighter tints. But not a leaf has fallen; they want the first whisper of the frost, and then they will go out like the lamps when the dawn breaks on a long festival.' On the hill to the north Mrs Disraeli had a 'German Forest' laid out, and decorated the terrace (where politicians enjoyed pacing to and fro) in the 'Italian style', placing Florentine vases filled with blue agapanthus there. Peacocks also roamed the terrace while on the lake majestic swans made a picturesque focus.

In 1877 Queen Victoria honoured Disraeli by visiting Hughenden. Victoria further honoured her favourite Prime Minister by having a memorial erected to him in the Church of St Michael and All Saints, in the grounds – it is unique in that it is the only monument erected to a subject by a reigning monarch. You can still see the small posy of primroses sent by the queen to Disraeli's funeral (protocol prevented her attending) in the manor along with a number of other personal items. There are locks of 'dear Dizzy's hair' lovingly labelled by his wife and the last pen he used.

Silver caskets contain the Freedom of the Cities of London and Glasgow. There is little of value financially – the Disraelis were always in debt – but there's plenty of interest. Look out for the side of a carriage surprisingly positioned like a piece of furniture. The story goes that Disraeli's wife trapped her finger in its door on the way to hear her husband make an important speech; she hid her pain which impressed Disraeli so much that he ordered the offending door to be preserved!

Practical details

Hughenden Manor, Great Missenden Rd, Nr High Wycombe, Bucks. (0494) 32580.

Admission charge (National Trust).
Open Apr–Oct 14.00–18.00 Wed–Sat, 12.00–18.00 Sun & Bank Hols; Mar 14.00–18.00 Sat & Sun.
Disabled facilities access limited to ground floor (four rooms) and grounds only; braille leaflet available.

Other facilities shop, toilets, parking, picnicking allowed in park.
Rail Marylebone to High Wycombe (40mins), then bus.
Coach Green Line to High Wycombe (1hr) then bus.
Nearby Bekonscot (10 miles), Oxford (25 miles).

TREAT!

A few miles from Hughenden, in West Wycombe, you can visit the interesting 'haunt' of the Hell Fire Club – a group of important and wealthy men who gained a dubious reputation during the late 18thC. Although suggestions that black magic was practised have not been substantiated, the fact that the 'Order' met in underground caves, and sometimes invited ladies to share the choicest wines with its members, was enough. It gained notoriety which was no doubt fuelled by one particular prank played by John Wilkes. Wilkes is said to have dressed a baboon up as a devil and hidden it in

Medmenham Abbey, where the club met. The baboon frightened Lord Sandwich who fled shouting, 'spare me, gracious devil, I am as yet but half a sinner, I have never been as wicked as I intended!' Wilkes was subsequently expelled from Parliament and imprisoned, but his career was not over and later, in 1774, he became Lord Mayor of London.

West Wycombe Caves, West Wycombe, Nr High Wycombe. (0494) 33739. Opening times vary. Please phone for details. Charge.

_____ *TREAT!*

ISLE OF WIGHT
85 miles S

Crossing the water to the Isle of Wight brings a marvellous sense of adventure and escape; and yet the journey from London is surprisingly quick and easily managed in a day. But you face two important decisions before setting out. The first is how to cross the Solent. There are a variety of options with car and passenger ferries leaving and arriving at different points on the mainland and island. For example you could sail from Lymington to Yarmouth, Southampton to Cowes, or Portsmouth to Fishbourne or Ryde. Do check which is the best route for you. The second decision is how to make the most of your time. The island that Karl Marx described as 'a little paradise', has grown into a much-visited tourist attraction and the choice of activities is quite bewildering. There are castles and chines, villas and vineyards, museums and mills, parks, potteries and pleasure boat trips. So it's worth planning your day in advance, whether you want to relax on one of the sandy beaches, take a long walk or cycle away from the tourist trail, or, if you prefer, an action-packed, sightseeing trip.

Although there are special offers on day crossings with a car, you can fit in a lot by using a Rover bus ticket giving unlimited travel for the day. Make sure you get a seat at the top as there are some lovely views on the way. A possible itinerary might begin by crossing from Portsmouth to Ryde on the Sealink high-speed catamaran service (15 minutes). From Ryde, you can catch a bus, via Newport, an old market town and capital of the island, to Carisbrooke with its famous Norman castle. This is a 'real' castle like those in kiddies' stories of medieval combat. Charles I was imprisoned here from 1647–8, the window where he got stuck trying to escape still in evidence, and visitors can quite literally follow in his footsteps by walking around the battlements. Once the king's morning exercise, the walk offers wonderful, windswept views. The island's County Museum is also housed in the castle, while queues always form outside the 16thC well-house where donkeys re-enact their ancestors' work treading a large wooden wheel to raise water.

The next stop is Yarmouth, a pretty town with a busy yachting harbour, pier and, tucked away down a side street, Yarmouth Castle, one of Henry VIII's coastal defences. There are picnic spots overlooking the harbour, but if you fancy a pub lunch then make for the Bugle Inn on the square. Continue your trip on to Alum Bay where the sand from the coloured cliffs comes in 20 or more different shades – and there are numerous souvenirs filled with sand to prove it! For a small fee, a chairlift will take you 165ft (50.3m) down to the beach, but for the sure-footed there are also steps. The chalky pinnacles of the Needles are the major attraction. For a close-up look you can take a boat trip out from the beach; but the restored Old Needles Battery, built in the 1860s and reached by a rather hairy cliff-top walk, has a 60ft (18.3m) tunnel leading to by far the most dramatic views.

If time allows, enjoy a refreshing cup of tea or light meal at the Alum Bay Tearooms before heading back to Ryde and across the water.

Practical details

Isle of Wight Tourist Office, Quay Store, Town Quay, Newport. (0983) 524343. Open 08.30–17.00 Mon–Thur, 08.30–16.30 Fri. This is an administrative centre only but will supply details of local Tourist Information Centres where personal callers are welcome.

Southern Vectis Omnibus Company, Nelson Rd, Newport. (0983) 522456. For information on Rover and other bus services.

Carisbrooke Castle, Carisbrooke. (0983) 522107. Open mid Mar–mid Oct 09.30–18.30 Mon–Sun; mid Oct–mid Mar 09.30–16.00 Mon–Sun. Charge (English Heritage).

The Needles Pleasure Park, Alum Bay. (0983) 752401. Open Apr–Oct 10.00–17.00 Mon–Sun (to 19.00 Sun & Wed end Jul–early Sep). Charge for rides.

Yarmouth Castle, Yarmouth. (0983) 760678. Open Apr–Sep 09.30–18.30 Mon–Sat, 14.00–18.30 Sun. Charge (English Heritage).

Rail and ferry Waterloo to Portsmouth to Ryde Esplanade (2hrs 20mins). For information on all Sealink Isle of Wight crossings phone (0705) 827744.

Coach National Express Victoria to Portsmouth Harbour (2hrs 30mins).

Nearby Beaulieu (10 miles), Portsmouth Naval Base (6 miles).

TREAT!

As a reminder of your island outing why not take home some freshly caught fish? Puffin Fisheries in Yarmouth is the place to go for a good choice. If you fancy crab or lobster then you can select your own; they keep them live in special tanks and will cook them on the premises and pack them ready for you to take away.

Puffin Fisheries, Saltern Wood Quay, Yarmouth. (0983) 760090. Open Apr–Sep 09.00–17.00 Mon–Sun; Oct–Mar 09.00–17.00 Tue–Sat.

TREAT!

KNEBWORTH HOUSE, GARDENS AND PARK

30 miles N

It comes as a surprise to many visitors that there's no sign of Knebworth House along the long drive to the entrance to Knebworth Park. Even as you pass through the gate all that's apparent is rough and wooded grassland stretching far into the distance. The 250-acre (101.3ha) park offers plenty of rambles among the herds of red and sika deer, but those in search of the house must drive on – passing on the right, the strange sight of a stockade. Here, within timber posts and towers, is the hugely popular Adventure Playground with Fort Knebworth, the Suspension Slide, Astroglide, Konkord Kastle and other activity equipment.

Then suddenly the house comes into view – a riotous assembly of Gothic fantasy with turrets, domes and gargoyles making up the extravagant façade. But you're in for a surprise because, behind the exterior, lies one wing of the original Tudor house. Knebworth House has been the home of the Lytton family since 1490 and each generation has left its mark on the rooms creating a real mixture of style and mood. The Jacobean Banqueting Hall with its 17thC oak screen and Minstrels' Gallery is particularly beautiful, and was a favourite with Charles Dickens who performed private theatricals here. Every historic house worth its salt must be able to boast at least one royal visitor. Knebworth is no exception: the Queen Elizabeth Room sports a magnificent four-poster bed where, tradition has it, Elizabeth I spent a night in 1588.

Of all the occupants, the two men who had the greatest influence on the house and gardens were Edward Bulwer-Lytton, the romantic Victorian novelist best known for *The Last Days of Pompeii*, and the architect Sir Edwin Lutyens who married into the family in 1897. The former re-created the house as a

Victorian palace, transforming both the exterior and interior. The State Drawing Room, the masterpiece of the eminent artist and designer John Crace, is a showcase of High Gothic decoration and furniture, but it's the Library that is the real tribute to Bulwer-Lytton. Over 70 volumes of his novels, plays, poems and essays line the walls. Sir Edwin Lutyens, on the other hand, set about simplifying the house. The White Drawing Room with its plain white panelling and family portraits is in keeping with the Edwardian style. Guides, who take visitors on tours of the house on weekdays, explain the history of the different rooms. At weekends there are attendants on duty.

The formal gardens at the rear of the house are currently undergoing a programme of restoration to reinstate as much as possible of the Edwardian layout favoured by Lutyens, while still maintaining the Victorian 'wilderness' with natural planting of trees, grass and flowers. Among the many points of interest is the herb garden, a unique quincunx pattern of circular beds designed for Knebworth in 1907 by artist Gertrude Jekyll, but only recently planted out after the drawings were discovered in 1980.

If time allows there are plenty of other things to do. Visit the fascinating exhibition and audio-visual display commemorating the Vice-Royalty of India of Lord Lytton and the great Delhi Durbar of 1877; travel on the narrow-gauge railway (charge) or explore the nearby Church of the Virgin Mary and St Thomas of Canterbury, filled with monuments to the Lytton family.

Practical details

Knebworth House, Knebworth, Herts. (0438) 812661.

Open mid Mar–mid May 12.00–17.00 house and gardens, 11.00–17.30 park Sat & Sun, Bank Hols & school hols; mid May–mid Sep same times Tue–Sun; end Sep–early Oct same times Sat & Sun only. Closed Mon except Bank Hols.
Admission charge.
Disabled facilities access limited to grounds and ground floor of house.

Other facilities free car park, toilets, gift shop, restaurant, café, picnic area, special events.
Rail King's Cross to Stevenage (30mins) then bus.

Coach Green Line Victoria direct (1hr 20mins). Operates mid May–mid Sep only.
Nearby Hatfield (10 miles), St Albans (15 miles).

TREAT!

A visit to Knebworth can be combined with Shaw's Corner in the pretty little village of Ayot St Lawrence. The home of George Bernard Shaw from 1906 until his death in 1950, the Edwardian villa has been imaginatively restored and presents an intriguing insight into his everyday life. The rooms have been left virtually unaltered and contain his personal belongings including, of course, his distinctive hats.

Shaw's Corner, Ayot St Lawrence, Nr Welwyn. (0438) 820307. Open Apr–Oct 14.00–17.30 Wed–Sat, 12.00–17.30 Sun & Bank Hols. Charge.

TREAT!

KNOLE
25 miles SE

A score of music seems a good metaphor to describe arrival at Knole. An unprepossessing gateway off Knole Lane signals your arrival. This relatively insignificant entrance is followed by a sweeping drive through the grounds which seems to gradually build up into a crescendo as you reach the top of the hill, and arrive at the house – the seat of the Lord of the Manor. Though decimated by the storm of October 1987, the 1000-acre

(405ha) deer park is ideal for walking and nature study but it is the house which deserves the closest attention.

Knole is vast, largely due to the demands and needs of King Henry VIII who stayed here while he was courting Anne Boleyn at nearby Hever Castle. Henry had appropriated Knole from the See of Canterbury while Cranmer, an ardent supporter of the Reformation, was Archbishop. It was next held, for a brief period, by Elizabeth I's favourite Lord Leicester. Then later, in 1566, it was given by the queen to her cousin Thomas Sackville – beginning a family occupation which still continues today.

Areas open to the public include the original main entrance through the West Front (described by Horace Walpole as having 'a beautiful, decent simplicity which charms one'). You then pass through two lovely courtyards, the Green Court followed by the Stone Court, into the Great Hall. Though much altered, the Great Hall is part of the original 15thC building built by Thomas Bourchier, Archbishop of Canterbury, in 1486. Next you ascend to the first floor up the Great Staircase, which is a cantilevered structure with mainly grisaille painted decoration dating from 1605–8. Upstairs there's an enormous amount to look at including an impressive Cartoon Gallery which houses six large copies of Raphael's cartoons; the Reynolds Room, named after the collection of paintings by Sir Joshua Reynolds which it contains; the Spangled Bedroom, so-called because of the patterned bed drapes; an impressive ballroom, with fine early 17thC panelling and decoration; and an important collection of 17thC furniture. Most splendid of all the rooms on show is, undoubtedly, the recently restored King's Bedroom. It took painstaking conservation, over a period of 13 years, to re-create the stunning fabric of the bed drapes. These gold and silver hangings are complemented by lavish silver furniture of a type rarely seen in Britain, making a triumphant climax to a visit to Knole.

Practical details

Knole, Sevenoaks, Kent. (0732) 450608.

Open Apr–Oct
11.00–17.00 (last
admission 16.00) Wed–Sat
& Bank Hol Mons (some
extra rooms open Fri).
Admission charge for
house (National Trust),
deer park free.
Disabled facilities access to
deer park only.

Other facilities shop,
toilets, free parking.
Rail Charing Cross to
Sevenoaks (30mins) then a
short walk to Knole.
Nearby Hever (8 miles),
Penshurst Vineyards (10
miles), Whitbread Hop
Farm (14 miles).

TREAT!

If you fancy spoiling yourself at lunch time, you
might like to sample the fare at the Royal Oak
Hotel. The set menu is changed daily and features
such dishes as mousseline of sweetbreads with
Nouilly Prat and fennel sauce for starters, then
maybe supreme of salmon with saffron sauce to
follow.

Royal Oak Hotel, Upper High St. (0732) 451109.
Lunch served Sun–Fri.

TREAT!

LEEDS CASTLE
40 miles E

It's a pity that you can't see Leeds Castle from the air,
because only from there can its beautiful setting and
picturesque moat be fully appreciated. Sadly, the next
best view of the castle's setting (the one used in many
of its brochures) is available only to golfers. Still, even
if you don't play golf or have access to a private plane
there is plenty of open space left for you to explore and
undoubtedly lots to see.

Unlike many historic houses and castles, Leeds keeps its car-parking area well away from its building, so a visit begins with a long and varied walk through the grounds. First comes the Duckery where the waterfowl have right of way and you must keep to the set path! It's a great hit with small children who are always enthralled by the other inhabitants of this section, the majestic and stunningly coloured peacocks. Continue on into the aptly named Woodland Garden. Initially landscaped in the 1920s, the Woodland Garden was conceived as a spring garden and if you visit early in the year you'll be treated to a pretty display of daffodils and narcisse, set amongst ash, willows and alder.

As the wooded area tapers out, the castle approach becomes apparent and you can see the Inner and Outer Barbicans and the site of the drawbridges. You then cross the moat (a lake fed by the River Len), pass through the Gate Tower (originally Norman but extended by Edward I in the 13thC) and enter the Inner Bailey. Entrance to the castle is via a circuitous but pleasant route which ends round behind the kitchen area. Indeed, the first thing you'll see on entering the castle is its wine cellar, which is one of the surviving sections of the castle built by Robert De Crèvecoeur during the early 12thC (although the Leeds Castle vineyards were recorded in the Domesday Book in 1086).

Inside the main section of the castle, rooms open to the public include Les Chambres de la Reine – a re-creation of two rooms as they might have looked in the 15thC; the Queen's Gallery, which boasts a fine oak ceiling; the Henry VIII Banqueting Hall; the Chapel; and a Seminar Room which houses a collection of Impressionist paintings with works by Degas, Pissarro and Vuillard.

On leaving the moated area of Leeds Castle, don't miss the opportunity to see the Culpepper Garden, the Aviaries and the Maze-Grotto. You can then cross a small bridge and walk back towards the car park along the far side of the Great Water which has an unusual view back to the castle.

Practical details

Leeds Castle, Maidstone, Kent. (0622) 65400.

Open Apr–Oct
11.00–17.00 Mon–Sun;
Nov–Mar 12.00–16.00 Sat
& Sun.
Admission charge.
Disabled facilities partial
access to castle; good
access to grounds.

Other facilities shop, café,
garden centre, free car
park, picnic area (by car
park), toilets.
No public transport
Nearby Canterbury (16
miles), Knole (25 miles),
Whitbread Hop Farm (27
miles).

TREAT!

In the village of Leeds you can visit the beautiful
church of St Nicholas which has close ties with
Leeds Priory. The advowson of St Nicholas's was
given to the priory by Robert De Crèvecoeur who
had founded the priory in 1119. It became the
richest Kent house of Augustinian Canons before
the Dissolution. A traditional Kent cobbled way
leads from the road to the tower, the church's most
memorable feature – an impressive, squat structure dating from early Norman times.

St Nicholas's Church, Leeds. Open most reasonable times.

TREAT!

LOSELEY HOUSE AND FARM
25 miles SE

Say the name Loseley and most people immediately
think of ice-cream, and here at Loseley Farm they
would be right! There are about 500 head of cattle on
the Loseley estate and in the milking parlour between
300–400 gallons of milk are produced daily – all of
which is processed into cheese, yogurt or the famous

Loseley ice-cream. Visits by the public to the farm take the form of a guided tour on which you see the herd of Jersey cows and rare breeds of sheep as well as pigs, peacocks and poultry. If you take a tour in the afternoon you will see the milking parlour in operation (at other times there is a full explanation and the chance to examine the equipment at close quarters). These tours can last up to two hours, so comfortable shoes are essential. However, for the less energetic there is an alternative way to make the same tour of the farm – on the back of a trailer pulled by a tractor!

The house is quite a contrast to the farm, though once again a visit is by guided tour and the guides have been known to be quite ferocious towards visitors who fail to pay attention or who look at items not being described. The house was built in 1562, at a total cost of £1640, by Sir William More, an ancestor of the present owner. Its stone façade is even older as it was brought from the ruins of Waverley Abbey near Farnham. Other salvaged architectural details include the panelling of the Great Hall which came from Henry VIII's Nonsuch Palace – the palace was built for Katherine Parr, and one of the panels has her initials inscribed on it. The initials of Queen Elizabeth I can be seen in the Library where they commemorate her visits to Loseley. Perhaps the most arresting room is the Drawing Room which is dominated by a chimney piece carved from a solid block of chalk to the designs of Holbein. Beside it you can see two Elizabethan maid of honour chairs whose cushions are thought to have been worked by Queen Elizabeth herself. Upstairs several principal bedrooms are on view including Queen Elizabeth's Room and the King's Room, so-called because it was used twice by King James I.

Practical details

Loseley Park, Guildford, Surrey. (0483) 571881. 24hr information service (0483) 505501.

Open house end May–Sep 14.00–17.00 (last   admission 16.30) Wed–Sat & Bank Hol Mons. Farm

tour Apr–Oct Mon–Sat.
Advance booking
required.
Admission charge
(separate for house and
farm).
Disabled facilities access to
grounds and ground floor
of house only.

Other facilities shop,
restaurant, free car park,
children's play area, picnic
area, toilets.
No public transport
Nearby Birdworld (12
miles), Wisley (8 miles).

TREAT!

A couple of miles away is the aptly named Inn on
the Lake. Here, you can enjoy a barbecue beside
the lake, weather permitting. But if the weather is
inclement, there's no need to worry as the inn's bar
boasts a real log fire and, perhaps even more
alluring, real ale. (Incidentally, the Inn on the
Lake's owner was voted Innkeeper of the Year
1986–7 and was given the Catey Award 1987–8.)
And you won't be disappointed if you try the
restaurant which has three fixed-price menus,
changed regularly, and a thoughtful wine list which
aims to represent the classic wine regions of
Europe.

Inn on the Lake, Godalming. (04868) 5575/6.
Restaurant open 12.00–14.00 & 19.00–22.00
Mon–Sun. Booking necessary for dinner.

_____ TREAT!

MEDIEVAL JOUSTING AT BELVOIR CASTLE
100 miles N

The grounds of historic Belvoir Castle provide the
perfect setting for this journey back in time to the days
of heroic knights and their brave chargers. Sitting on
the grassy hillside in front of the castle you're treated to

all the thrills of the medieval joust. It certainly makes a spectacular and most unusual afternoon's entertainment; one particularly enjoyed by foreign visitors. The event is introduced by the Joust Master who acts as both referee and compère throughout. He explains the rules and then welcomes the knights and war horses, all dressed in traditional jousting costume. There's the dastardly Black Knight who believes the only rules are his own, Sir Malcolm of Roxburgh, good and true, Sir Guy of Goscote, Sir Richard of Gloucester and others – each a great character and an impressive horseman.

An important feature of the medieval joust was that knights would be fighting for a lady's favour. At Belvoir that tradition continues. Ladies in the audience are asked to hold up hankies or scarves so that each knight may choose a lady to represent. With the selected favour tied to his lance he will then fight to prove himself in the owner's eyes. The knights are divided into two teams and take part in two tournaments, both lasting 35 minutes. First there's a series of skilful one-to-one combats with the knights scoring points for their teams. This is followed by the individual challenges between personal rivals. Tempers run high and the atmosphere gets so tense at times it's hard to believe it's only a re-enactment. As the crowd

Jousting at Belvoir Castle

starts cheering and hissing, you can't help but be swept along in the general excitement.

The second part of the tournament is the Grand Mêlée, an all-in battle between the two teams with the knights dressed in full armour. Each one is armed with his favourite weapon (thankfully, blunted) which could be a sword, an axe, a ball and chain, or perhaps a mace. With the support of their men-at-arms, the knights charge at each other, some on horseback, some on foot. The frenzy of fighting continues until the bitter end when the victors are jubilant, the vanquished exhausted and the crowd stand to cheer the valiant efforts of all.

As Belvoir Castle is quite a way from London, it's worth packing as much into the day as possible, so do spend some time in the castle and grounds. The castle, home of the Duke and Duchess of Rutland, dates back to Norman times but the present building is largely mid 19thC. It is packed with interest and you may well need more than one visit to see and absorb everything. Among the items of special interest are the art treasures which include works by Poussin, Rubens and Reynolds; the exquisite tapestries, Chinese silks and fine porcelain; and a bugle used at 'The Charge of the Light Brigade' in 1854, on display in the military museum. The castle gardens, studded with 17thC statues, are planted so there's something in flower throughout the year. But perhaps the most striking feature of all is, as the name Belvoir (though pronounced Beever) suggests, the stunning view over the surrounding vale.

Practical details

Belvoir Castle, Grantham, Lincs. (0476) 870262.

Open Medieval Jousting Tournaments held on selected days. Write or phone for details. Castle open mid Mar–end Sep 12.00–18.00 Tue–Thur & Sat, 12.00–19.00 Sun, 11.00–19.00 Bank Hol Mons; Oct 12.00–18.00 Sun only. *Admission* charge (included in entrance fee to castle). *Disabled facilities* access

can be arranged. Contact in advance.
Other facilities free car park, toilets, gift shop, café and picnic area. No dogs except guide dogs.
Rail King's Cross to Grantham (65mins), then taxi (7 miles).
Nearby None of the other attractions included in this book is within 25 miles of Belvoir.

TREAT!

The Vale of Belvoir is dotted with delightfully unspoilt villages so if you're travelling by car, why not take a slight detour from the main roads to discover them for yourself. If you fancy a bite to eat, the village of Knipton has a very good pub, the Red Lion, which attracts customers from miles around. The village church, largely 13thC, is well worth a visit. The parson is usually chaplain to the castle.

The Red Lion, Knipton. (08015) 611.

TREAT!

THE NATIONAL HORSERACING MUSEUM AND EQUINE TOURS
63 miles NE

It was Charles II who established Newmarket as the centre of British horseracing. A frequent visitor, he revelled in the challenge of a two-horse race across the glorious heath, and the town's tradition as headquarters of the 'sport of kings' is still embodied in the fine buildings of the prestigious Jockey Club. With such an equine history it comes as no surprise to find a museum devoted to racing – but you might be surprised to find it so fascinating. The museum is full of interest even to the complete novice, with displays on horses and courses, classic races, famous jockeys and trainers. You can find out how the rules of the sport were established and about the rigours of life as a jockey. There are plenty of easily digestible snippets of information, some remarkable stories and even more intriguing scandals.

The museum also organises tours of Newmarket and relics of its racing tradition. There are a number of different tours varying in length from 2½ hours to a full day. The content obviously depends on the time factor, but you're asked if there's anything you'd particularly like to see right at the start which adds a pleasant personal touch. The season will have an influence too – in the spring, the young foals are a lively sight; in summer there's the fairground atmosphere of the racing season; and in the late autumn, the sales take place at Tattersalls where thoroughbreds are bought and sold and millions of pounds change hands.

From the museum, a most well-informed and friendly guide takes you on a tour of places of equine interest in and around Newmarket, home to a staggeringly high 2250 racehorses. You will spend time watching the splendid spectacle of horses being put through their paces on the gallops, the traditional training ground. As paintings in the museum show, the sight has changed little in over 250 years. This is a chance to talk to some of the trainers who come to check on their horses' performance, and to the stable lads (whatever their age or sex, they're still called lads), to get a few hot tips and hear a few tales. You're also shown around one of the typical training yards; and on a longer tour there's a visit to the National Stud, one of the principal stallion centres in Britain. Here, you meet some of the great stallions and find out about the precious care and incredible expense involved in breeding thoroughbreds. The whole tour is a real eye-opener.

Practical details

The National Horseracing Museum and Equine Tours, 99 High St, Newmarket, Suffolk. (0638) 667333.

Open museum early Apr–early Dec 10.00–17.00 Tue–Sat,	14.00–17.00 Sun. Closed Mon except Bank Hols. Tours operate on same days.

Booking essential for tours.
Admission separate charge for museum and tour.
Disabled facilities access to museum. Contact in advance to arrange tours (a guide can accompany you in your own car).

Other facilities free car park, toilets, gift shop, café, garden.
Rail Liverpool Street to Newmarket (1hr 36mins).
Coach National Express Victoria to Newmarket (2hrs 45mins).
Nearby Cambridge (14 miles), Ely (16 miles).

TREAT!

Don't leave Newmarket without drooling over the delicious fare in Musks, a delicatessen with a huge assortment of luxury foods. Their speciality is home-made sausages, by Appointment to Her Majesty Queen Elizabeth, the Queen Mother.

Musks, 1 The Rookery. (0638) 661824. Open 09.00–17.00 (to 13.00 Wed) Mon–Sat. Closed 13.00–14.00.

TREAT!

NEW FOREST
85 miles SW

The name 'New Forest' is really rather misleading. It's certainly not new – dating back to before the 11thC, when William the Conqueror enclosed this vast area as his first Royal Hunting Ground. Nor can it be accurately described as a forest. Of the 90,000 acres (36,450ha), nearly a third is open heathland and bracken. However, one thing for certain is that the New Forest is absolutely enchanting and it is also one of the few places where you can still see England as it was in medieval times.

With an area as large as the New Forest, one of the best ways to explore is by car. The many landscaped car parks, dotted around in places of beauty or interest, make the forest an ideal place for a day's drive stopping off now and again for a walk or picnic. However, motorists should note that the roads are narrow and do get congested in the summer. So if you possibly can, try to plan your visit at an off-peak time – perhaps in the early spring when the New Forest bursts into life with foals and beautiful flowers, or in the autumn when the heathland and trees are rich with glorious colour.

To make the most of your visit, call first at the New Forest Museum and Visitor Centre in Lyndhurst, ancient capital of the forest. Here, you'll find maps, trail leaflets and also displays highlighting the story of the forest, its many traditions, legends, characters and the abundance of wildlife. The forest is so varied that every visitor will want to discover their own favourite parts, but there are several features which should be included and can easily be covered in one day. Among these are two historical points of interest: the Knight-wood Oak, gnarled and wizened, which is over 400 years old and the oldest surviving tree in the forest; and the Rufus Stone at Brook, which commemorates the spot where William Rufus (William II, son of William the Conqueror) died in 1100. The spectacular Rhine-field Ornamental Drive (ornamented by trees) is probably best avoided in the height of the season, but on a less crowded day it makes a superb sight. This drive leads to the Tall Trees Walk, a waymarked route through an avenue of lofty trees planted in 1860. And as an unexpected contrast to the heaths and woods, Lymington Town and Quay is a bustling sailing centre on the seafront.

The forest is noted for its ponies and you can see them wandering everywhere with a disturbing disre-gard for motorists. You may even find yourself coming to a complete halt as the ponies 'shade'. They often collect in large groups and then stand on three legs and happily doze off. They appear to be awake, but there's no way you can budge them, so wait patiently until a Forestry Commission Ranger gets them moving! To avoid accidents to the ponies, all the main roads are fenced and visitors are asked not to feed or attract them onto the road. Less obvious, but equally famous, are the deer. These shy, reserved animals tend to hide from visitors, but you can watch the lightfooted fallow deer in the Deer Sanctuary from the observation point at Bolderwood. And mention must also be made of the forest pigs. In the spring they lie on the greens with their suckling piglets, and then during the 'pannage' season from September to November, when they are allowed to pasture in the forest, they can be seen scurrying in the undergrowth for acorns. The pigs are there to eat the acorns which would otherwise kill the ponies – a tradition which dates from medieval days.

Practical details

Lyndhurst Tourist Information Centre, High St, Lyndhurst, Hants. (042128) 2269. Open Apr–Oct 10.00–18.00 Mon–Sun.

The New Forest Museum and Visitor Centre, High St, Lyndhurst. (042128) 3914. Open Apr–Oct 10.00–18.00 (to 20.00 Aug) Mon–Sun; Nov–Mar 10.00–17.00 Mon–Sun. Closed Christmas Day.

Rail Waterloo to Brockenhurst (1hr 30mins).
Coach National Express Victoria to Lyndhurst via Southampton (2hrs 40mins).
Nearby Beaulieu (2 miles), Broadlands (10 miles).

TREAT!

Right in the heart of the forest at Emery Down is the New Forest Inn which started its life as a hostelry back in the 1700s, when you didn't need a licence to sell beer. Apparently, a trader sold beverages from a caravan on the site and that caravan still forms the basis of the front porchway and one of the bar walls. Today, it's a very comfortable pub offering accommodation and serving excellent bar snacks including the speciality of the region, venison sausages.

The New Forest Inn, Emery Down. (042128) 2329.

TREAT!

NORWICH
100 miles NE

The climb up to the viewpoint on St James Hill is pretty steep, but it's worth persevering – from the top of the hill there's a fine view of the layout of this ancient city with its narrow streets, medieval churches and old buildings all clustered around the cathedral whose tall, elegant spire is second in height only to Salisbury. Founded in 1069 by Herbert de Losinga, apparently as a penance for his sins, Norwich Cathedral is noted among many things for the grave of Nurse Edith Cavell who was shot by a German firing squad in Belgium in 1915 for her part in helping British soldiers to escape. A simple and melancholy sight, the grave is by a wall in the south transept. Displays in the cathedral's visitors' centre tell more about the life of Edith Cavell and also highlight the history of the building and its many other points of interest.

Opposite the cathedral is Tombland Alley where many victims of the Great Plague are buried, and a short walk away stands the great keep of the Norman castle. The castle overlooks Market Place, where a weekly market still thrives. The stalls (their awnings are known locally as 'tilts') sell everything from the weird and wonderful to the mundane, and the traders maintain a stream of jovial patter. The City Museum is now housed in the castle and boasts a superb collection of the Norwich School – paintings commissioned by wealthy, local families in the late 19thC. Nearby in old Bridewell Alley, a medieval shopping street, there are two completely different museums. The Bridewell was built as a merchant's house in the late 14thC and used as a prison from 1583–1828. It is now a museum of rural crafts and local industries with exhibits including the Norwich Shawls which were so popular with Queen Victoria and often appear in her photographs. The Mustard Shop is home to a museum packed with pots, pictures and recipes depicting the history of Colman's mustard over 150 years. You might think this is an extraordinary subject for a museum, but the displays are most absorbing – take particular note of the story of the Mustard Club, one of the most successful advertising campaigns ever. The shop itself has been restored and redecorated in Victorian style with period fittings and furnishings and sells an incredible variety of mustards.

Another museum worth a visit is Strangers' Hall in Charing Cross, named after the immigrants from the Netherlands who settled in the city in the 16thC. This late-medieval merchant's house has room sets furnished in period from early Tudor to the late Victorian times. And if only for the sheer prettiness of its location on Elm Hill, don't miss the medieval church of St Peter Hungate, now a museum of ecclesiastical arts and crafts and a busy brass rubbing centre. This narrow flint-cobbled street is particularly charming at night when lanterns light the way, so prolong your trip to Norwich until the evening if you can.

Practical details

Tourist Information Centre, Guildhall. (0603) 666071. Open Jun–Sep 09.30–18.00 Mon–Sat, 09.30–13.00 Sun; Oct–May 09.30–17.30 Mon–Fri, 09.30–13.00 Sat.

Bridewell Museum, Bridewell Alley. (0603) 611277. Open 10.00–17.00 Mon–Sat. Charge.

Castle Museum. (0603) 611277. Open 10.00–17.00 Mon–Sat, 14.00–17.00 Sun. Charge.

Mustard Shop Museum, Bridewell Alley. (0603) 627889. Open 09.00–17.30 Mon, Wed, Fri & Sat, 09.30–17.30 Tue. Closed Thur & Sun. Free.

Norwich Cathedral, Tombland. (0603) 626290. Cathedral open Apr–Sep 07.30–19.00 Mon–Sun; Oct–Mar 07.30–18.00 Mon–Sun. Free. Visitor Centre open 10.30–16.30 Mon–Sat. Films shown on the hour in film room 11.00–16.00. Free.

St Peter Hungate Museum, Princes St. (0603) 611277. Open 10.00–17.00 Mon–Sat. Closed Sun. Free. Charge for brass rubbing.

Strangers' Hall Museum, Charing Cross. (0603) 611277. Open 10.00–17.00 Mon–Sat, 14.00–17.00 Sun. Charge.

Rail Liverpool Street to Norwich (1hr 55mins). *Coach* National Express Victoria to Norwich (3hrs 50mins).

Nearby None of the other attractions included in this book is within 25 miles of Norwich.

┌─ *TREAT!* ─────────────────────────────

Near to the castle is the Georgian Assembly House where fashionable families once gathered. Grand and luxurious, it's just the place to treat yourself to a cream tea or home-baked cake. The Assembly House is also open for morning coffee and lunches. An additional attraction besides the lovely decor, friendly staff and tasty food is the art or craft exhibition held on most days.

The Assembly House Restaurant, Theatre St. (0603) 627526. Open 10.00–19.30 Mon–Sat. Closed Sun & Bank Hols.

─────────────────────────── *TREAT!* ─┘

ORIENT EXPRESS

You can step back in time to the 1930s on board the Orient Express. The railways were in their heyday then and, for those privileged people who could afford it, travel was unashamedly luxurious. A trip today is no less expensive but, for opulence, atmosphere and a sense of occasion, it's hard to beat. Pullman cars, which once provided the rich and famous (including royalty) with comfortable travel, have been restored and are now back on the tracks.

There are a number of day excursions available including trips to Leeds Castle, Bath, Hever Castle, Broadlands and Beaulieu – all of which are featured in this book. Each excursion does differ slightly, but they all include travel to and from the destination, champagne, lunch with wine, a guided tour, and tea. You have to do nothing except enjoy yourself.

A typical trip might be to Goodwood House. Once on board and settled into comfortable, individual, lace antimacassar-covered armchairs, and even before the train has moved away from Victoria Station (where the Orient Express has its own platform), champagne and orange juice is served. A continental breakfast with more Buck's Fizz soon follows and the miles quickly begin to fly by. Most passengers take the opportunity to freshen up, and it's a chance which shouldn't be missed – on board the Orient Express even this is an experience!

When you get off the train you are given a few minutes in which to have your photograph taken standing beside the train, perhaps with an ever-friendly, crisply uniformed steward. Then it's onto the waiting coach for the short road journey to Goodwood House. There follows a private tour of Goodwood, not perhaps one of England's finest country houses, but then there isn't much time to see it anyway. After a superficial introduction to some of its better paintings, including works by Canaletto and Stubbs, it's time for a sherry reception in the highly attractive Yellow Drawing Room. Sherry is quickly followed by a good (bearing in mind that the kitchens are catering for at least 100 diners) three-course lunch. Once lunch is over it's time to return to the train for tea. There's another chance to freshen up, admire the marquetry, and take a few more photographs – just to prove you really have been on board the famous Orient Express.

Practical details

Venice Simplon Orient Express, Sea Containers House, 20 Upper Ground, London. (01) 928 6000. Times and dates of excursions vary so please phone for information.

Disabled facilities none.
Other facilities meals served on board and at destination (special diets catered for – please advise in advance), souvenirs available, special treats (such as flowers and birthday cakes) may be ordered in advance, toilets.
Nearby Not applicable.

┌─ TREAT! ──────────────────────────────────┐

If you really want to travel in style and to enter into the spirit of the occasion, why not dress up in a 1930s costume? Suitable clothes can be hired from many London costume-hire shops, including the biggest of them all, Bermans & Nathans.

Bermans & Nathans, 18 Irving St, London WC2. (01) 839 1651.

TREAT! ┘

OXFORD
56 miles W

Oxford, like Cambridge, is famed for its university. It's impossible to avoid Matthew Arnold's 'dreaming spires' and William Wordsworth's 'domes and towers', and to miss pretty polychromatic Keble College or historic Christchurch Cathedral would be a real pity. However, there's plenty in the city for the tourist to see and do without ever venturing into any of the colleges.

If you're a keen museum visitor, Oxford should be something of a mecca. The most famous is definitely the world-renowned Ashmolean which boasts great masters from all periods of European painting, plus an important print collection and a coin department which is considered second only to that of the British Museum. There's also a fascinating Egyptian collection and a beautiful selection of oriental ceramics.

Less well known but equally worth a visit is the Pitt Rivers Museum. Its collection of ethnographic material includes children's milk teeth and shrunken heads; needless to say, the Pitt Rivers is a popular choice with youngsters. It is well hidden behind the University Museum, which is a place worth browsing in as much for its Victorian Gothic architecture as its collection of fossils, bones and gem stones. Leaving the past behind and coming up to date, take a look at the

Museum of Modern Art. MOMA's changing exhibitions of contemporary art can be exciting and its café is recommended.

Oxford also enjoys many outdoor attractions like the Botanic Garden, the oldest 'teaching garden' in the country. It was started in 1621 as a physic garden where plants were grown for medical and scientific uses. Today the plants are grouped with an eye to their relationships within the plant world – which nevertheless still manages to be aesthetically pleasing, particularly after the hurly-burly of the adjacent High Street. The garden spreads out beside famous Magdalen Bridge where great crowds gather on May Morning to hear choristers sing from the top of Magdalen College Tower: they mark the start of the May Day celebrations – bell ringing, morris dancing and a terrible crush of people (many the worse for alcohol).

Finally, do try your hand at Oxford's most romantic activity – punting. Evocative of ages past, punting is both a pleasure and an art; you don't have to wear a boater or a flowing white dress, nor do you have to trail a bottle of wine in the cooling waters of the River Cherwell – but it certainly helps!

Practical details

Oxford Tourist Information Centre, St Aldates. (0865) 726871. Open end May–Aug 09.00 (09.30 Tue)–17.30 Mon–Sat, 10.30–13.00 & 13.30–16.00 Sun, Bank Hols & Tue following Bank Hol; Sep–end May 09.00–17.30 Mon–Sat. Closed Sun.

Ashmolean Museum, Beaumont St. (0865) 278000. Open 10.00–16.00 Tue–Sat, 14.00–16.00 Sun, 14.00–17.00 Bank Hol Mons. Free.
Botanic Garden, High St. Open mid Mar–mid Oct 08.30–17.00 Mon–Sat, 10.00–12.00 & 14.00–18.00 Sun; mid Oct–mid Mar 09.00–16.30 Mon–Sat, 10.00–12.00 & 14.00–16.30 Sun. Glasshouses open 14.00–16.00 Mon–Sun. Free.
Christchurch College Cathedral, St Aldates. Open 09.00–17.00 Mon–Sat, 13.00–17.00 Sun. Charge.
Keble College, Parks Rd. Open 10.00–dusk Mon–Sun. Free.

Magdalen College, High St. Open 14.00–18.15 Mon–Sun. Charge.
Museum of Modern Art, 30 Pembroke St. (0865) 722733/728608 (recorded information). Open 10.00–18.00 Tue–Sat, 14.00–18.00 Sun. Charge.
Pitt Rivers Museum, Parks Rd (entrance through University Museum). (0865) 270927. Open 14.00–16.00 Mon–Sat. Free.
University Museum, Parks Rd. (0865) 272950. Open 12.00–16.00 Mon–Sat. Free.
Rail Paddington to Oxford (45mins).
Coach National Express Victoria to Oxford (1hr 30mins); Oxford Tube Victoria to Oxford (1hr 30mins).
Nearby Blenheim Palace (10 miles), Cotswold Wild Life Park (17 miles), Hughenden Manor (25 miles).
Note colleges may close without notice.

TREAT!

Queues regularly form outside Browns restaurant – an eating place which has been extremely popular for years with tourists, students and locals alike. Babylon fans, parquet floors and tall potted plants set the atmosphere, enormous salads and steaming dishes like Beef and Guinness Pie do the rest.

Browns, 5–9 Woodstock Rd. (0865) 511995. Open 11.00 (12.00 Sun)–23.30 Mon–Sun.

TREAT!

PENSHURST VINEYARDS
32 miles SE

Even if you are not a wine enthusiast Penshurst has something to offer. For youngsters there are animals – rare breeds of sheep, numerous wallabies and exotic water fowl including black swans and Indian runner ducks; for adults there is the opportunity to learn about the process of wine making and enjoy a tasting session. The atmosphere around the vineyard is friendly and remarkably easygoing for a commercial enterprise. Individual visitors are welcome to roam about at will; free to walk amidst the growing vines, into the winery and through the animal enclosures.

Organised groups can book a guided tour which covers both the tradition of wine making in England (which dates back to Roman times) and the history of wine growing at Penshurst. There's an explanation of the growing of various varieties of grape vines which here include Müller Thurgau, Scheurebe, Reichensteiner and Seyval Blanc. Then it's into the most modern winery in England to discover how some 60,000 bottles are produced each year. You will be shown the grape press, bottling equipment, wine filter and labelling machinery. Finally, there's the part of the tour which by now everyone is waiting for with some anticipation – the tasting of the wine produced here, which is all white.

Both individuals and groups can take advantage of the picnic site at Penshurst which has a fine view over a pretty part of the Kent countryside and, to round off the visit, can buy a bottle of wine made from the fruits which surround them.

Practical details

Penshurst Vineyards, Grove Rd, Penshurst, Kent. (0892) 870255.

Open Apr–Oct 10.00–18.00 Mon–Sun; Nov–Mar 10.00–16.00 Mon–Sat.
Booking advance booking essential for guided tours. Duration 1½-2hrs. Minimum 15 people.
Admission individuals free, charge for guided tours (children free).
Disabled facilities access.

Other facilities free car park, picnic tables, gifts, toilets, free wine tasting. No dogs allowed.
No public transport
Nearby Hever Castle (8 miles), Knole (10 miles), Whitbread Hop Farm (12 miles).

┌ *TREAT!*

For a traditional afternoon tea try Fir Tree House
Tea Rooms. Waitress service and a partially 16thC
setting add to the enjoyment of home-baked cakes
and scones and delicious granary bread.

Fir Tree House Tea Rooms, Penshurst. (0892)
870382. Open Apr–Oct 15.00–18.00 Tue–Sun.
Open Bank Hols but closed Tue after.

TREAT! ┘

POOLE AND BROWNSEA ISLAND
100 miles SW

A quick look at a map shows the extent of Poole
Harbour, one of the largest natural harbours in the
world. A mecca for lovers of watersports, it's awash
with colour and activity during the summer season with
sailors, windsurfers and waterskiiers coming from
miles around to show off their skills competitively or
purely for pleasure. Indeed, locals argue that you can
probably see every type of boat at Poole Harbour from
tall ships to fishing boats, and cross channel ferries to
the flat-bottomed canoes specially designed for the
shallow waters around Sandbanks.

Scheduled boat trips leave regularly from the quay.
There's a choice of trips including a tour of the harbour
and a journey up the River Frome to the pretty Ware-
ham Quay, but most interesting of all is a boat trip
across to Brownsea Island.

The trip lasts around 10–20 minutes and takes you
around the harbour with Sandbanks on your left,
widely recognised as one of the cleanest beaches in
Britain. The boat lands at the entrance to Brownsea
Castle, built by Henry VIII but considerably altered in
the 19thC. The castle isn't open to the public, but the

500-acre (202.5ha) island, owned by the National
Trust, has a wealth of interest with scenic walks across
heaths, through grassland and woodland, and is an
ideal habitat for wildlife including many peacocks.
There are also family beaches and wooded glades
providing perfect picnic spots. The island is famous as
the place where Baden-Powell first organised an ex-
perimental Scout Camp in 1907, the start of the scout-
ing movement. A stone which marks the spot also
offers a lovely view across to the Purbeck Hills with the
ruins of the great Corfe Castle peeping through the
gap. The northern half of the island is a nature reserve,
managed by the Dorset Trust for Nature Conservation, and can be visited either by guided tour or on a
self-guided trail. The island is best known for its colony
of rare red squirrels, heronry and herd of sika deer, but
it also attracts many ducks and waders, and nesting
common and sandwich terns.

When planning a boat trip remember to save enough
time to see some of the attractions in Poole itself. Poole
is perhaps most famous for its pottery but you'll also
find some unusual museums, an impressive aquarium,
a busy park and award-winning family beaches.

Practical details

Poole Tourism Centre, Poole Quay. (0202) 673322.
Open Jan–Mar 09.00–17.00 Mon–Fri, 10.00–16.00 Sat
& Sun; Apr–Jun 09.00–17.30 Mon–Sun; Jul–early Sep
09.00–21.00 Mon–Sun; end Sep–Dec 09.00–18.00
Mon–Fri, 10.30–17.00 Sat & Sun.

Brownsea Island open
Apr–Sep 10.00–19.00 (or
dusk) Mon–Sun. Charge
(National Trust).
*Brownsea Island Nature
Reserve*, The Warden
(0202) 70774. Dorset Trust
for Nature Conservation
(0202) 707745. Guided
tours Apr, May, Jun &
Sep 14.45 Tue, Thur, Sat,
Sun & Bank Hols; Jul &

Aug 14.45 Mon–Sun.
Charge.
*Harvey's Pleasure Boats of
Poole Harbour*, Enefco
House, Poole Quay.
(0202) 674063/675563.
Departures from either
Fish Shambles Steps,
opposite Poole Pottery, or
The Ferryway,
Sandbanks.

Open Apr–Sep at regular intervals. *Admission* charge. *Disabled facilities* access. *Other facilities* toilet, running commentary throughout trip. *Rail* Waterloo to Poole (2hrs).	*Coach* National Express Victoria to Poole (2hrs), Excelsior Coachways King's Cross to Poole (2hrs). *Nearby* Beaulieu (24 miles), Weymouth (25 miles).

TREAT!

Like so many of the best pubs, the King Charles Inn in Poole has a resident ghost to add that extra something to the olde-worlde atmosphere. Affectionately known as Freda, she's said to roam the 15thC Kynges Halle which adjoins the main bar. Whether or not you meet Freda, this is the place to go for a lunchtime drink and fresh seafood meal or snack.

King Charles Inn, Thames St. (0202) 67450.

TREAT!

PORTSMOUTH NAVAL BASE
70 miles S

Old, historic battleships and new, modern warships lie side by side at Portsmouth's Naval Base. Still operational and extremely busy, the base, which has been the home of the Royal Navy since Henry VII first founded the Royal Dockyard, is a fitting resting place for a unique collection of historic vessels. And to provide the historical context for these great ships, the Royal Naval Museum is also housed at the base.

The museum, set in a series of Georgian storehouses, tells the story of the Royal Navy from Tudor times right up to the South Atlantic Campaign. Among the many different exhibits is a collection of the relics

HMS *Victory*

of Admiral Lord Nelson who sailed from Portsmouth
with the English fleet in a campaign that resulted in the
famous Battle of Trafalgar in 1805. There's an exciting
panorama of the battle, complete with very dramatic
light and sound effects. Nelson's flagship, HMS *Victory* is berthed outside. This proud survivor of the
celebrated naval confrontation is now beautifully preserved and a fine example of the heyday of the great
wooden sailing warship.

Resting in a dry dock workshop close by, is the hull
of the warship *Mary Rose*, pride of Henry VIII's fleet.
Built here at the naval base in 1509–10, then sunk on its
way out of the harbour in 1545, her hull was raised
amid a blaze of publicity in 1982. Visitors are welcome
to view the hull and admire the ongoing and painstaking work involved in its conservation and reconstruction. Queues do tend to be rather long, especially at
the height of the summer season, but it's well worth the
wait. Before seeing the remains of the great ship, you
may find it helpful to visit the Mary Rose Exhibition,
housed in a converted Georgian masthouse just a short
walk away. This exhibition explains not only the amaz-

ing series of events leading up to the raising of the *Mary Rose*, but also illustrates the importance of its discovery as a time-capsule of life at sea in the 16thC. Exhibits of objects recovered from the ship help build up a vivid and very revealing picture of the seafaring past.

The latest arrival at the base is HMS *Warrior*. Launched in 1860, *Warrior* was Britain's first iron-hulled, armoured battleship and soon became the largest, fastest, best-protected and most formidable warship of its time. Walking on board is like stepping back to the 1860s. Everything has been so well re-created, right down to the crockery on the mess table, that it feels almost as though the crew have just gone ashore. In keeping with this 'real-life' atmosphere, there are no information boards, but uniformed quarter-masters are happy to answer any questions.

Practical details

Portsmouth Naval Base Maritime Heritage Attractions. (0705) 839766/750521. Open 10.30–17.00 (17.30 Mar–Oct) Mon–Sun. Closed Christmas Day. Last admission 30mins before closing.

Admission free.
Disabled facilities access and toilets.
Other facilities souvenir shops, toilets, café and picnic areas.
HMS Victory. (0705) 839766. Open as for naval base but closed 10.30–13.00 Sun. Charge.
HMS Warrior. (0705) 291379. Open as for naval base. Charge.
Mary Rose. (0705) 812931/839766. Open as for naval base. Charge (ticket covers entry to the hull and to the exhibition).

Royal Naval Museum. (0705) 733060. Open as for naval base but closed for a week at Christmas.
Rail Waterloo to Portsmouth Harbour (1hr 35mins).
Coach National Express Victoria to Portsmouth (2hrs 30mins).
Nearby Broadlands (25 miles), Goodwood (24 miles), Isle of Wight (6 miles), Weald and Downland Open Air Museum (25 miles).

┌─ *TREAT!* ─────────────────────────────────┐

About a 15-minute walk from the naval base are
the fortifications at Old Portsmouth, built in Tudor
times to defend the harbour entrance and protect
the Royal Dockyard. The Round Tower, built in
1418 and the oldest of the defences, offers a quite
spectacular view over the Solent. The observation
roof is open all the time, free of charge, and there
are plenty of benches so you can sit and enjoy the
panorama at your leisure.

Old Portsmouth fortifications, Old Portsmouth
High St.

TREAT!
└───┘

RYE AND WINCHELSEA
68 miles SE

Today Rye is a pretty, cobbled hill town, several miles
from the sea, and a favourite haunt of Sunday painters.
But back in the 14thC it was a very different place.
Significantly, it was a walled coastal town (the sea has
since retreated) and, far from being a picturesque
haven, was a thriving smuggling port. Smugglers' tales
abound, but perhaps nowhere more so than in the
Mermaid Inn. There's been an inn here since 1156, but
marauding French burnt down the original building
and the building you see today dates from 1420. Smugglers are said to have felt so secure in The Mermaid
that they openly traded their contraband there.
However, they did have the safeguard of numerous
hiding places within the inn's labyrinth, and in the Snug
Room for instance there's a hinged bookcase which
opens to reveal a secret space.
   Rye is now a delightful, romantic place to wander
around. Half-timbered medieval dwellings, Elizabethan buildings and Georgian houses all cluster

together in the tranquil area surrounding St Mary's Church. Another more unusual structure, looking rather like a brick tea-caddy, can be found on the east side of Church Square. In fact this beautiful building is an 18thC water tower.

A short walk from the church is the Ypres Tower, now a local museum but built in the mid 13thC by Henry III to fortify Rye. Steps beside the tower lead into a public garden which boasts a formidable view over Romney Marsh to the Channel. Some of the cannon used in Elizabethan times to defend Rye now ornament this pleasant open space.

A visit to nearby Winchelsea provides a dramatic contrast to the disorganised delights offered by Rye. Not that Winchelsea is unattractive, and its historic ambience is equally powerful, but it is quite a surprise to find such an ancient settlement laid out on a grid pattern. Winchelsea was devised by Edward I's planners to replace the earlier Winchelsea which had been washed away by the sea. They based their design for a new town on a chequer-board pattern. By keeping to this rigid grid system, they created a place which to us seems surprisingly modern. Incidentally, most of the façades you can see date from the 18thC when the town was 'brought up to date'.

At the heart of Winchelsea stands the lovely, serene church of St Thomas's. Its interior, beautifully dappled by coloured light which streams from its stained-glass windows, is unusual in that it has three altars immediately visible. Other unexpected details abound: look out for medieval carved heads; a 17thC carved statue of Our Lady and Holy Child; and several tombs including that of Gervase Alard – appointed Admiral of the Western Fleet by Edward I.

Practical details

Tourist Information Office (for Rye and Winchelsea), Cinque Port St, Rye, Sussex. (0797) 222293.

Mermaid Inn, Mermaid St, Rye. (0797) 223065.

Rye Museum, Ypres Tower, Gun Garden, Off

Church Sq. (0797) 223254.
Open Apr–mid Oct
10.30–13.00 & 14.15–
17.30 (last admission
17.00) Mon–Sun. Charge.
St Thomas's Church, St
Thomas's St, Winchelsea.

Closed during services.
Rail Charing Cross to Rye
via Ashford, Kent (1hr
30mins).
Nearby Battle (12 miles),
Great Dixter House (8
miles).

┌ *TREAT!*

When you're near the sea, fresh seafood often
becomes something of a 'must'. Rye abounds with
places to eat, but the family-run Flushing Inn has
achieved a special reputation for seafoods. Fresh
crab, Rye Bay plaice and the astoundingly named
'Agglomeration of Crustaceans and Molluscs' all
feature on the lunchtime menu and you could try
'A Rye Rouser' to round it off. Incidentally, if
you're wondering about the origins of the name
Flushing, no one knows for sure. The most likely
theory is that Flushing is a corruption of the old
English word for butcher – 'flesher' – and somehow
Fleshers' Inn became Flushing Inn.

Flushing Inn, Market St. (0797) 223292.

TREAT! ┘

ST ALBANS
20 miles NW

Under the Romans St Albans was known as Verulamium and was one of the most important towns in their
western empire. To find out what it was like to live in
this municipium around AD43, make for the Verulamium Museum. This informative collection is packed
with finds from local exacavations – mosaics, pottery,
pins, tacks, painted plaster – but most helpful of all the
exhibits is probably the large model of the Roman city.

When you've absorbed its layout, and noted which sections can still be seen, it's time to do some exploring. First visit the Roman theatre – it's the only one of its kind in Britain which has a stage rather than an amphitheatre. Next take a walk through Verulamium Park, where large sections of Roman wall can be seen along the Causeway, and nearby you can see a hypocaust which has been preserved.

Today St Albans is an attractive town whose historic streets present an architectural medley. Look out for the Marlborough Almshouses (Hatfield Road), the Georgian Bleak House (Normandy Road) and the Fighting Cocks Inn (Abbey Mill Lane). The inn takes its name from the cruel sport of cock fighting for which it was once a well-known centre, but the building is thought to have originally been a fishing lodge for the abbey. The abbey cannot, and should not, be missed. Along with the Cathedral Church it dominates St Albans and all routes seem to lead to it. The abbey is said to mark the site of the execution of St Alban – Britain's first Christian martyr (executed in AD209).

Finally, if you're visiting on a Saturday or Wednesday do browse around the market (well worth viewing from the top of the clock tower). Trading has taken place here since AD948 when Ulsin, Abbot of St Albans, was granted permission to hold a market. It was held on the then open ground between Chequers Street, French Row and High Street. Over the centuries the stalls became the permanent buildings which can be seen today.

Practical details

Tourist Information Centre, 37 Chequer St. (0727) 64511. Open 10.00–17.00 Mon–Fri, 10.00–16.00 Sat.

Clock Tower, Chequer St. Open Apr–mid Sep 10.30–17.30 Sat & Sun. Charge. *Roman Theatre*, off Bluehouse Hill. (0727) 35035. Open 10.00–17.00 (16.00 Oct–Mar) Mon–Sun. Charge. *St Albans Abbey and Cathedral Church*. (0727) 60780. Open 07.00–18.45 (17.45 Oct–Mar) Mon–Sun. Closed during services.

Verulamium Museum, St
Michael's St. (0727)
54659. Open Apr–Oct
10.00–17.30 Mon–Sat,
14.00–17.30 Sun;
Nov–Mar 10.00–16.00
Mon–Sat, 14.00–16.00
Sun. Charge.

Rail St Pancras to St
Albans (20mins), King's
Cross to St Albans (times
vary).
Nearby Hatfield House (5
miles), Knebworth (12
miles).

TREAT!

If you're feeling hungry after your exploration of
the past, try Waffles. In the unusual setting of a
water mill which is thought to date from Elizabethan times, a range of tasty sweet and savoury
waffles are dished up in cramped, but friendly,
style.

The Waffle House, Kingsbury Water Mill, St
Michael's St. (0727) 53502. Open Apr–Sep 11.00–
18.00 Wed–Sun; Oct–Mar 11.00–17.00 Wed–Sat,
12.00–17.00 Sun.

TREAT!

SALISBURY
90 miles SW

If you choose to travel to Salisbury by car your route
will take you past the ancient site of Old Sarum which
has been in its time an Iron Age hill fort, a Roman
settlement, a Saxon burgh, a Norman motte, castle and
town, and the site of the first Salisbury Cathedral. In
the 13thC, due to lack of water and space and after a
dispute with Richard I, the church authorities moved
their cathedral to a new site on the flat plain and Old
Sarum was gradually abandoned. The City of New
Sarum (as Salisbury is officially known), situated on
fertile land, quickly expanded into a regionally import-

ant trading centre which still thrives today. Look out for Poultry Cross in Butcher Row – 600 years old, it still provides shelter for traders from the lively produce market which now flourishes over Market Square, where the Salisbury Charter Fair is held every October.

The city is, of course, famed for its cathedral, acknowledged as the most attractive of all those in Britain. Both its appearance and outstanding setting were memorably captured by the brush of John Constable. (If you want to see what the artist saw you can follow in his footsteps across the meadows along Town Path to Harnham Mill.) Built between 1220–58 this Gothic triumph has a unique unity of proportion. It also boasts a spire (added a hundred years later) which rises some 404ft (123.2m) above the ground, making it the highest in England and the third highest in Europe. In the aisle there's a fascinating clock mechanism dating from 1386, while in the Chapter House you can see one of the three originals of the priceless Magna Carta signed at Runnymede on 15 June 1215. The area around the cathedral, known as Cathedral Close, has a picture-book quality. It is the largest close in England and contains buildings which date from the 13thC to the present day. One of the grandest houses is King's House, now the award-winning Salisbury and South Wiltshire Museum. Displays illustrate the development of Salisbury from the settlement of Old Sarum to the modern city of today. You can also find out about ceramics, early man and the world-famous ancient monument, Stonehenge.

Salisbury is also peppered with interesting churches like St Martin's in Tollgate Road, whose foundations pre-date that of the cathedral and whose spire is thought to have been built to practise the techniques later used for constructing the cathedral's spire. And don't miss the Church of St Thomas A'Becket in St Thomas Square. This is the parish church of Salisbury. It was founded by the builders of the cathedral and contains a remarkable painting of Doom over its chancel arch. Hell is depicted as the mouth of a large fish

which swallows up the damned, while the redeemed
rise from their tombs and Christ sits on a rainbow.

Practical details

Tourist Information Centre, Fish Row. (0722) 334956.
Open Apr–Sep 09.00–19.00 Mon–Sun; Oct–Mar
09.00–17.00 Mon–Sat, closed Sun.

Old Sarum (2 miles N of
Salisbury, off A345).
(0722) 335398.
Open mid Mar–mid Oct
09.30–18.30 Mon–Sat,
14.00 (09.30 Apr–Sep)–
18.30 Sun; mid Oct–mid
Mar 09.30–16.00 Mon–Sat,
14.00–16.00 Sun.
Admission charge.
Disabled facilities access to
inner bailey and grounds
only.
Other facilities toilets,
parking.
Access car, local bus
(phone (0722) 336855 for
details), or on foot
walking beside River
Avon (phone (0722) 20379
for details).
Produce Market, Market
Sq. Open Tue & Sat.

*Salisbury and South
Wiltshire Museum*, 65 The
Close. (0722) 332151.
Open Apr–Sep 10.00–
17.00 Mon–Sat, 14.00–
17.00 Sun (Jul & Aug
only); Mar–Oct 10.00–
16.00 Mon–Sat, closed
Sun. Charge.
Rail Waterloo to Salisbury
(1hr 27mins).
Coach Green Line
Victoria to Salisbury (2hrs
30mins), National Express
Victoria to Salisbury (2hrs
30mins).
Nearby Broadlands (16
miles), Hawk
Conservancy (16 miles),
Stourhead Gardens (22
miles).

TREAT!

Harper's 'Shoppers' Special', is a good-value
three-course lunch which is very popular with
locals and tourists alike. Harper's certainly lives up
to their boast that real food 'home-made and
wholesome' is their speciality. A generous bowl of
soup, followed by a huge steak and kidney pie like
granny used to make, accompanied by vegetables
bought in the market outside, then an enormous
portion of apple crumble, is typical of its fare.
All in all, it's an excellent place for a mid-day

refuelling to prepare yourself for an afternoon seeing the sights!

Harper's, Market Sq. (0722) 333118. Open 12.00–14.00 & 18.30–22.00 (to 22.30 Sat) Mon–Sat. Vegetarian and children's menus available. Essential to book for a table with a view over the market.

_____ *TREAT!*

THE SHUTTLEWORTH COLLECTION
45 miles N

The spectators' stunned silence says it all – the flying displays at Old Warden Aerodrome are quite breathtaking. There are no thrills and spills, no stunts or daredevil antics, just the remarkable sight of historic aeroplanes taking to the air against the backdrop of Bedfordshire countryside. A favourite to watch is the 1912 Blackburn monoplane which has the distinction of being the oldest British aeroplane still flying. However, all the aeroplanes in the displays, many of which are part of the permanent Shuttleworth Collection, hold a special interest whether it's the 1917 S.E.5a, a British fighter plane which can reach the speed of 140mph, or the impressive Gloster Gladiator, the last of the biplane fighters. Flying days are only held during the summer months when weather conditions allow but the collection, housed in seven hangars, is open nearly every day throughout the year giving the opportunity for a closer look at the aircraft. Everyone who enjoyed the film *Those Magnificent Men in their Flying Machines* will love the collection. At this wonderfully old-fashioned aerodrome, just a couple of miles from the busy A1, time seems to stand still as the 30 or so planes recall the history of aviation – from a Blériot monoplane of the type used by the Frenchman to make the first cross-Channel flight between Calais

Shuttleworth Collection

and Dover, in July 1909, to the spectacular World War II Spitfire.

Although aeroplanes are the main attraction, there's also a garage full of road vehicles, all in good working order. Among the highlights is the 1898 Panhard Levassor which Richard Ormonde Shuttleworth, the founder of the collection, first drove in the London–Brighton run in 1928 and which is still wheeled out at regular intervals. The display of vehicles ranges from steam cars to fire-engines, bone-shakers and tricycles to early motor cycles. And on show in the coachroom are some magnificent horse-drawn carriages. You'll need time to enjoy the collection to the full, but do make sure you save at least half an hour for a visit to Hangar 1 where you can see the engineers at work restoring and repairing the aeroplanes. The collection was begun in 1928 with the intention that everything should continue to work in the same way as it did when it was first made. It's the achievement of that aim over the years, that makes the Shuttleworth Collection so special.

Practical details

The Shuttleworth Collection, Old Warden Aerodrome, Biggleswade, Beds. (0767) 27288.

Open 10.00–17.00 (16.00 Nov–Mar) Mon–Sun.

Closed for a week over Christmas & New Year.

Last admission 1hr before closing. Telephone for details of special events. *Admission* charge. *Disabled facilities* access. *Other facilities* car park, gift shop, toilets, restaurant, children's playground.

Rail King's Cross to Biggleswade (35mins) and then taxi for 3 miles. *Coach* Whippet Coaches King's Cross to Biggleswade (1hr 20mins) and then taxi for 3 miles. *Nearby* Audley End (22 miles), Knebworth (16 miles), Wimpole Hall (16 miles).

TREAT!

Flour is still milled in the traditional way at Holme Mills on the River Ivel at Biggleswade. The mills, run by the Jordan family since 1855, are not open to the public, but there's a delightful shop selling flour, cereals and all sorts of nutritious goodies.

Mill Shop, Holme Mills. (0767) 312001. Open 09.00–17.00 Mon–Fri, 09.00–12.00 Sat.

TREAT!

SOUTH DOWNS WAY (BRAMBER TO WASHINGTON)
45 miles S

A brisk walk high up on the ridge of the lovely South Downs is a perfect pick-me-up; a day of freedom and fresh air far, far away from the pressures of office or home. You can really feel the gusty wind 'blowing away the cobwebs' as you follow the way-marked route past fields of grazing cattle, over stiles, through woods, along ancient trackways and past Neolithic settlements; with sweeping views before you and an abundance of wildlife around you. Obviously it depends on the time of year, but in early summer slopes of cowslips, orchids and the South Downs' own round-headed campion are a joyful sight, while the cheery sound of the stonechat and fleeting visits from beautiful butterflies bring interest at every step.

The South Downs Way was the first of the country's designated 'Long Distance Bridle-paths' – a trackway for walkers, cyclists and horse-riders. It stretches some 80 miles across the crest of the chalky Downs between Eastbourne and the cliffs of Beachy Head in the east, and Harting and Buriton in the west. It should ideally be tackled in a week but with a car and a bicycle or companions and two cars, you can easily cover one section in a day. All you need is an Ordnance Survey map, a compass and sensible clothing – sturdy shoes are a must, and as there's little shelter from the sun, rain and changeable winds you're well advised to dress accordingly.

Local tourist information centres have booklets outlining the different sections of the way to help you plan your route. A particularly pleasant walk covering about 6½ miles takes you from Bramber to Washington. First leave one car or your bicycle at the free car park in Washington, then drive on to Bramber where there's another free car park. A public footpath takes you along the River Adur past the abandoned medieval village of St Botolphs to join the South Downs Way. Now follow the signs which are refreshingly unobtrusive. The words 'South Downs Way' and the acorn symbol of the Countryside Commission are displayed on oak signs, concrete plinths, gates and fences. The path climbs Annington Hill which overlooks the ancient market town of Steyning and then you continue with the distinctive oval shape of the remains of the Iron Age fort at Cissbury on your left. Further on is Chanctonbury Ring, a clump of beech trees planted in the 18thC on the site of a prehistoric hill fort, and a famous landmark and viewpoint. The Way now guides walkers over the A24 to continue to Amberley and beyond, but take a diversion into Washington for some well-deserved refreshment before cycling or driving back to pick up the car at Bramber. You can get a good, hearty meal at the local pub at Washington which welcomes weary walkers – but not their muddy boots!

Practical details

South Downs Way, East and West Sussex.

South East England Tourist Board, 1 Warwick Park, Tunbridge Wells, Kent. (0892) 40766. Open 09.00–17.30 Mon–Thur, 09.00–17.00 Fri. Will supply information on all stages and all aspects of the walk.
Admission the walk is free but admission is charged to many of the attractions along the route.

Facilities car parks, cafés, pubs and restaurants in villages and towns along the route.
Nearby Brighton (8 miles), Goodwood (22 miles), Weald and Downland Open Air Museum (25 miles), Wildfowl Trust, Arundel (15 miles).

TREAT!

A far cry from the fresh air of the Downs admittedly, but if you feel up to tackling a museum then the House of Pipes in Bramber is well worth a visit if only to meet the extrovert and immensely entertaining founder, Anthony Irving. His collection, built up over 40 pipe-smoking years, is devoted to smoking and all its side-kicks with pipes, postcards, coupons, cutters, matches and much more.

House of Pipes, Bramber, West Sussex. (0903) 812122. Open 09.30–18.30 Mon–Sun & eves by arrangement. Charge.

TREAT!

STOURHEAD GARDENS
110 miles SW

Imagine a valley whose steep sides are covered with a variety of mature trees, all looking fresh, green and healthy. Then add to the image bright splashes of colour – orange, yellow, purple, pink and red. Now imagine a large blue lake at the heart of the valley, which reflects all the colours surrounding it and the clouds above. Finally, conjure up thoughts of classical Greek temples and place them in this verdant, valley setting. The picture you have created is that of Stourhead Gardens during the spring.

Begun in 1741, the gardens were designed for Henry Hoare II, the son of a wealthy banker. The graceful lake was created by damming medieval fish ponds, then over the decades its sides were planted with trees and shrubs from all over the world. A lovely circuit walk, which is still followed today, was set out and along its route several buildings were constructed. These were based on those Hoare had seen while on his Grand Tour. Following this 18thC walk you pass the Temple of Flora, designed in 1744 by architect Henry Flitcroft and the first building to be erected in the gardens. Then, in contrast, there's an eerie grotto which dates from 1748. Nearby there's a Gothic cottage whose origin is uncertain but which was certainly a later addition to the garden. Next on the route is the Pantheon, perfectly positioned on the lakeside to provide a stunning focal point for the garden. Interestingly, it was once heated through brass grilles. The last of the garden buildings, the Temple of Apollo (a copy of the round temple excavated at Baalbec in the Lebanon), is only reached after a stiff climb, but it's well worth the exertion for the view alone. Other things of interest to be enjoyed on the walk include the Turf Bridge, a copy of Palladio's bridge in Vicenza; the Bristol High Cross which dates from the 15thC; an ice house; a cascade; and an obelisk.

Stourhead Gardens

After the extraordinary beauty of Stourhead's gardens, its house may come as rather an anticlimax. Nevertheless, designed in 1725 by Colen Campbell and based on a Palladian villa, it is considered to be one of the prototype English country houses of the 18thC and as such it's worthy of attention.

Practical details

Stourhead House and Gardens, Stourton, Warminster, Wilts. (0747) 8403348.

Open house Apr & Oct 14.00–18.00 Sat–Wed; May–Sep 14.00–18.00 Sat–Thur. Last admission 17.30. Closed Nov–Mar. Garden open all year 08.00–19.00 (or dusk if earlier) Mon–Sun. No dogs allowed Mar–Sep.
Admission separate charge for house and garden (National Trust).
Disabled facilities access to most of the garden good, entrance to house difficult (flight of stairs and staff instructed not to help with wheelchairs), but interior all on one level.
Other facilities shop, toilets, café, picnicking, meals at Spread Eagle Inn (within grounds), free car park.
Rail Waterloo to Gillingham (2hrs) then taxi (4 miles).
Nearby Avebury (20 miles), Bath (15 miles), Salisbury (22 miles).

┌─ *TREAT!* ─────────────────────────────────

Garden lovers can enjoy an entirely different sort of garden at neighbouring Stourton House (shares Stourhead car park and is reached by a two-minute walk through a farmyard). Stourton has the same soil as Stourhead, but there the similarities end. This is a small (4 acres – 1.62ha), private, intimate garden with the emphasis on informality. It is also designed to provide dried herbaceous flowers which are on sale to the public.

Stourton House, Stourton. (0747) 840417. Open Apr–Nov 11.00–18.00 (or dusk if earlier) Wed, Thur, Sun & Bank Hol Mons. Charge.

─────────────────────────── *TREAT!* ─┘

STRATFORD-UPON-AVON
80 miles W

Every year thousands of tourists flock to Stratford to learn more about one man, William Shakespeare. Much of the town's attraction lies in its association with this famous Elizabethan playwright. You can explore his wife's picturesque thatched dwelling which is known as Anne Hathaway's Cottage. Cottage is however something of a misnomer as it is actually a 12-roomed farmhouse, the home of a substantial yeoman family. In Wilmcote, three miles from Stratford, you can visit another Tudor farmstead. This is where Shakespeare's mother lived as a child and is known as Mary Arden's House. The neighbouring Glebe Farm is now a countryside museum open to the public. For most people, however, it is Shakespeare's Birthplace which makes a trip to Stratford special. This attractive half-timbered Elizabethan house has been divided into two; one half is furnished to re-create the sort of environment Shakespeare may have experienced, and

Anne Hathaway's Cottage

the other half is devoted to a display which illustrates his life and works.

Two other buildings are associated, though rather more tenuously, with the dramatist – Nash's House and Hall's Croft. In the garden of the former, which belonged to Thomas Nash the first husband of Shakespeare's grand-daughter, you can see the site and foundations of New Place, the house where Shakespeare died in 1616. Hall's Croft was once the home of his daughter Susanna and her husband Dr John Hall; today it contains an exhibition illustrating medicine during the 17thC while its beautiful walled garden offers a tranquil haven for the footsore visitor.

But there is no reason, unless you are a total devotee, to visit all the Shakespeare properties. It is perhaps best to choose just one or two and then enjoy some of the other sights Stratford has to offer. One prominent feature of the town is the River Avon which is flanked by gardens and a recreation ground. A pretty bank-side walk will take you past a brass rubbing centre (particularly popular with children) and on to .Holy Trinity Church where Shakespeare is buried. Alternatively you could take a look at the river from a boat. An atmospheric steamboat chugs down the waterway taking in some typically beautiful Warwickshire scenery en route, or those feeling more romantic (and energetic!) might prefer to hire a punt and pole gently past one of Britain's most famous playhouses – the Royal Shakespeare Theatre.

Practical details

Tourist Information Centre, Bridge St. (0789) 293127. Open Apr–Oct 09.30–17.30 Mon–Sat, 14.00–17.00 Sun; Nov–Mar 10.00–16.00 Mon–Sat, closed Sun.

Anne Hathaway's Cottage, Shottery. (0789) 204016. Open Apr–Oct 09.00–18.00 (17.00 Oct) Mon–Sat, 10.00–18.00 (17.00 Oct) Sun; Nov–Mar 09.00–16.30 Mon–Sat, 13.30–16.30 Sun. Last admission 20 mins before closing time. Charge.

Hall's Croft, Old Town. (0789) 204016. Open Apr–Oct 09.00–18.00 (17.00 Oct) Mon–Sat, 10.00–18.00 (17.00 Oct) Sun. Closed Nov–Mar. Last admission 20 mins before closing time. Charge.

Holy Trinity Church, Southern Lane. Open 09.00–16.00 (or dusk) Mon–Sun. Closed during services. Charge.

Mary Arden's House and Shakespeare Countryside Museum (including Glebe Farm), Wilmcote. (0789) 204016. Open Apr–Oct 09.00–18.00 (17.00 Oct) Mon–Sat, 10.00–18.00 (17.00 Oct) Sun;

Nov–Mar 09.00–16.30 Mon–Sat. Closed Sun. Last admission 20 mins before closing time. Charge.

New Place/Nash's House, Chapel St. (0789) 204016. Open Apr–Oct 09.00–18.00 (to 17.00 Oct) Mon–Sat, 10.00–18.00 (17.00 Oct) Sun; Nov–Mar 09.00–16.30 Mon–Sat. Closed Sun. Last admission 20 mins before closing time. Charge.

Royal Shakespeare Theatre. Booking information (0789) 295623. Restaurant reservations (0789) 293226.

Shakespeare's Birthplace, Henley St. (0789) 204016. Open Apr–Oct 09.00–18.00 (17.00 Oct) Mon–Sat, 10.00–18.00 (17.00 Oct) Sun; Nov–Mar 09.00–16.30 Mon–Sat, 13.30–16.30 Sun. Last admission 20 mins before closing time. Charge.

Steamboat and boat hire, G. H. Rose & Son, Swan's Nest Boathouse (best reached via the footbridge). (0789) 67073. Open Apr–Oct 09.00–dusk Mon–Sun. Closed Nov–Mar. Charge. *Stratford Brass Rubbing Centre*, Avon Bank Garden, Southern Lane. (0789) 297671. Opening times vary so please phone for details. Charge. *Rail* Euston to Coventry (1hr 10mins) then coach/bus to Stratford (35mins). *Nearby* Warwick Castle (10 miles).

TREAT!

No visit to Stratford can really be considered complete without a night (or afternoon!) at the theatre. Before watching the play you can visit the Royal Shakespeare Company Collection which has over a thousand items connected with the company on view. These include props, costumes, pictures and old recordings, and traces the development of RSC productions over the years. You might also like to join a backstage tour and learn about the building and the present productions.

Royal Shakespeare Theatre, Stratford-upon-Avon. (0789) 296655. The times of the backstage tours vary depending on the performance schedule. Booking required. Collection open 09.15–19.30 Mon–Sat, 11.00–16.00 Sun. Charge.

TREAT!

THORPE PARK
21 miles SW

Aimed at family groups, but with roughly 6–14 year olds particularly in mind, Thorpe Park is a good solution for entertaining energetic youngsters. As the entrance fee covers all the rides (and that includes repeat

trips), there's no problem filling a day. Indeed, sometimes the park is so popular that you must spend the
day here if you are going to try all the most popular
rides because they inevitably have long queues.

The most breathtaking attraction must be Space
Station Zero, a fast and furious ride through swirling
coloured lights, made more frightening by the tilt of
the seats – hold onto your tummy if you brave this one!
The prize for wettest ride goes to Thunder River. This
is a fast flowing stretch of water on which circular craft
are launched: as they buffet against each other they
create huge splashes and everyone gets soaked (water-
proofs can be bought but you might consider taking
your own unless, of course, it is a gloriously hot day).
Other more sedate watery things to do include Water
Gardens Pedalos, Water Bus trips and Farm Ferry
which, as its name suggests, crosses the lake to Thorpe
Farm (popular with small children). For the healthy
and active there are plenty of ways to burn off some
energy and you could try whizzing round the Roller
Rink, where you can hire skates if you don't have your
own.

Small children are well catered for – there are a
selection of rides provided for those measuring 4ft 9ins
(1.45m) and under, and a Dizzy Den for those between
2ft 6ins–4ft 9ins (0.76–1.45m). Everyone is welcome
to experience Cinema 180, a nausea-producing piece
of cinematic technology (film projection is done onto a
half-domed surface), which allows you to actually feel
what it's like to ride on the Big Dipper – though,
unfortunately, at the time of research the film pro-
jected was rather worn so the result was not very
exhilarating.

A firm family favourite is a trip on board the
Treasure Island Railway. Here all credit for the fun
must go to the 'actors' playing the parts of train drivers
and pirates as it's their enthusiasm which makes (or
could break) this attraction. Another, entirely different, trip is Phantom Fantasia, and it doesn't take too
much guesswork to realise that this is the ghost train –
but don't worry, it isn't scarey at all!

Practical details

Thorpe Park, Staines Rd, Chertsey, Surrey. (0932) 562633.

Open end Mar–mid Apr (school hols) 10.00–18.00 Mon–Sun; mid Apr–May 10.00–18.00 Sat, Sun & Bank Hols; Jun–end Jul 10.00–18.00 Mon–Sun; end Jul–Aug (school hols) 10.00–20.00 Mon–Sun; early Sep 10.00–18.00 Mon–Sun; mid–end Sep 10.00–18.00 Sat & Sun. Last admission 16.00 (18.00 Aug). Closed Oct–end Mar. *Admission* charge (most rides/amusements included in entrance fee but occasional extra charges are made).

Disabled facilities access possible, but some limitation on rides. *Other facilities* café, restaurant, teas, picnic area, free cark parking, sweet shop, souvenir shops, camera hire kiosk, baby care, toilets. *Coach* Green Line Victoria to Thorpe Park (1hr 30mins). *Nearby* Bekonscot Model Village (16 miles), Chessington World of Adventures (8 miles), Windsor (20 miles), Wisley (10 miles).

TREAT!

Just a few miles away at Runnymede off the A328 is Magna Carta, the site of a very important event – the signing of the Great Charter by King John after his meeting with the barons at Runnymede on 15 June 1215. The Magna Carta subsequently became regarded as a milestone in British constitutional history. This historic site is marked with a small temple-like building behind which can be found several attractive walks.

TREAT!

WARWICK CASTLE
95 miles W

Ask any young visitor what they like best about Warwick Castle and the answer will come back, the
dungeons and the peacocks. While adults may not
share children's inexplicable delight in deep, dark,
places of torture, it's only too easy to be enchanted by
the lustrous colours of the numerous castle peacocks.
You may well be met in the car park by a rather
forward bird who will willingly accept a hand-held
titbit – you may even be treated to an ostentatious
display of distinctive blue and green plumage.

Inside the castle, picturesquely situated on the bank
of the River Avon, there's plenty to see and do. If
you're feeling energetic, you may like to climb to the
top of 128ft-high (39.1m) Guy's Tower. The breathtaking views over Warwickshire are well worth the effort
of struggling up and up, and round and round the spiral
staircase. You can also take a stroll along Rampart
Walk which boasts beautiful views, particularly over
the castle park and the town of Warwick. More climb-
ing will take you into the Clock Tower and Barbican
where there are some informative displays about the

Warwick Castle

Beauchamp Earls of Warwick and Warwick the 'King Maker'. Yet another tower, Watergate, is said to be haunted by the ghost of Sir Fulke Greville who was murdered in the castle in 1628 – sound effects tell of his unhappy demise. For a more leisurely and less gruesome walk, wander through the former private residential wing where a Royal Weekend Party of 1898 has been re-created. During the 1890s the Earl and Countess of Warwick held many house parties in the castle and something of their atmosphere has been recaptured with the help of life-like portraits in wax of 29 of the principal guests and their servants. They include HRH The Prince of Wales (later King Edward VII), HRH The Duke of York (later King George V), the Duke and Duchess of Devonshire and Winston Churchill. It's an effective insight into the former glory of the castle and its occupants.

The castle grounds, landscaped by Capability Brown, are very attractive and, depending on the season, you may see colourful displays of daffodils or rhododendrons. There's a re-created Victorian Rose Garden, laid out to the original designs (1868) of Robert Marnock, and a late 18thC conservatory.

Finally, if you want to find a peaceful spot for a rest, cross the footbridge over the Avon to River Island. This tranquil haven has dramatic views of the castle's river front which is over 400ft (122m) long and 120ft (36.6m) high.

Practical details

Warwick Castle, Warwick, Warks. (0926) 495421.

Open Mar–Oct 10.00–17.30 Mon–Sun; Nov–Feb 10.00–16.30 Mon–Sun. Victorian Rose Garden open Mar–Oct only. *Disabled facilities* no access. *Other facilities* restaurant, café, picnic area, car park, toilets, shops. *Coach* Green Line Victoria to Warwick (2hrs 30mins). *Nearby* Stratford-upon-Avon (10 miles).

┌─ *TREAT!* ─────────────────────────────

In Warwick town centre (a two-minute walk from the castle) you can visit a true Tudor treasure – the Lord Leycester Hospital. The hospital was founded in 1571 by Robert Dudley, Earl of Leicester as a retirement home for his aged retainers. Today visitors can admire the unique candle-lit Guild Chapel of St James, the fine Great Hall and the attractive, galleried courtyard. While in Warwick take a look at St Mary's in Church Street which contains a lovely medieval chapel. And if you're looking for somewhere for tea (the castle restaurant could not be recommended at the time of research), try Charlotte's which has delicious home-made cakes.

The Lord Leycester Hospital, High St. (0926) 492797. Open Apr–Sep 10.00–17.30 Mon–Sat, Oct–Mar 10.00–16.00 Mon–Sat. Closed Sun, Good Fri, & Bank Hols. Charge.
Charlotte's Tea Rooms, Jury St. (0926) 498930.

─────────────────────────────── *TREAT!* ┘

WATERWAYS MUSEUM AND CANAL TRIP
65 miles NW

The small Northamptonshire village of Stoke Bruerne on the banks of the Grand Union Canal was once a thriving centre for canal traffic. Its importance as a trading point is now long gone, but it's not difficult to imagine the days when barges would pull up at this canalside village and, the working day over, the boat-men would enjoy a well-deserved glass of beer. The setting is picturesque, the atmosphere friendly and, clustered around this small stretch of canal, there's a wealth of interest.

Waterways Museum

The Waterways Museum is housed in a converted
cornmill. Three floors of exhibits and displays help
conjure up a picture of the hard-working lifestyle of the
boatmen and their families. Don't miss the replica of
the cabin of the butty boat *Sunny Valley* complete with
kitchen range. A butty boat is one without an engine
and would have been pulled by motorboat or horse. It
is certainly brightly decorated, with collections of
porcelain 'lace' plates, horse brasses and painted ware,
but so cramped it's hard to believe a whole family could
live here. The museum looks at the history of inland
navigation over the last 200 years, while outside the
canal of today is waiting to be explored. After your
tour of the museum, equipped with all the background
knowledge, you can set off for the afternoon.

First, take a look at the double lock almost directly
opposite the museum and the boat weighing machine,
once used to check the correct toll charges. Just
beyond is a bridge offering splendid views of the
charming, thatched village of Stoke Bruerne. The
towpath passes beneath this bridge. To the south, lies
the flight of seven locks known as the Stoke Locks
leading to the village of Cosgrove. Going north, the
towpath takes you to the mouth of the Blisworth
Tunnel, one of the largest tunnels ever built and still in
use. Opened in 1805, it is a daunting 3086yds (2821m)
long. In the past, travelling through the tunnel was a

rather tricky operation. While the horses were walked over the hill, professional 'leggers' were employed at the rate of one old penny a trip to 'walk' the boat through. They would lie on boards, one on either side of the boat, with their feet up on the tunnel side and use their feet to push the boat through. Thankfully, nothing so energetic is expected of visitors taking a trip on the canal today. In fact, a 25-minute journey to the mouth of the tunnel is a thoroughly pleasant experience. Among the boats offering trips is *Indian Chief*, a 55ft (16.8m) purpose-built narrowboat with all mod-cons including a toilet, central heating and a well-stocked bar. As the boat gently meanders along at a leisurely pace, let your thoughts drift away too . . . a perfect end to the day.

Practical details

Waterways Museum, Stoke Bruerne, Nr Towcester, Northants. (0604) 862229.

Open Apr–Sep 10.00–18.00 Mon–Sun; Oct–Mar 10.00–16.00 Tue–Sun. Telephone to check. Last admission 30mins before closing.
Admission charge.
Disabled facilities access. Please give advance notice.
Other facilities car park, toilets, café and picnic facilities nearby, gift shop.
Indian Chief Cruises, Stoke Bruerne, Nr Towcester, Northants. (0604) 862428.

Booking telephone for details and times of departure. Longer trips can be arranged for parties of over 30.
Admission charge.
Disabled facilities access.
Other facilities toilet, bar, music and public address system, video, shop, picnic meals can be organised.
No public transport
Nearby Woburn Abbey and Wild Life Kingdom (24 miles).

TREAT!

Traditionally a 'watering-hole' for working boatmen, the Boat Inn on the waterfront opposite the museum is now a favourite stopping-off point for visitors to the canal. The bars boast a wide range of beers, bar snacks and pub games (you can even try your skills at the local game of hood skittles!) and there's also a licensed restaurant with an à la carte menu and a tea room serving light snacks.

The Boat Inn, Stoke Bruerne. (0604) 862428. Bars open 11.00–14.30, 18.00–23.00 Mon–Sun. Tea room times vary depending on the season and number of visitors. Please phone for details.

TREAT!

WEALD AND DOWNLAND OPEN AIR MUSEUM
60 miles SE

This open air museum is not only a fascinating insight into the rural past, but also quite simply a lovely place to be. Set in 40 acres (16.2ha) of beautiful Sussex countryside, the grounds contain a millpond, attractive woodland walks and plenty of picnic places where you can rest in between walking around the different buildings on display. However, it's definitely a museum where you need a guidebook to appreciate what's on show, so do buy the guide and study the map before setting off. The best place to start is the introductory exhibition showing the traditional regional building materials and methods. This is housed in a typical late-18thC barn from Hambrook in Sussex. Look out for the pictures showing how it was repaired and re-erected here at the museum.

  The aim of the Weald and Downland Open Air Museum is to provide a home for indigenous buildings from the south east of England which have either been left to fall into ruins or threatened with demolition. The museum, set against a backdrop of stunning scenery, has a representative medley of rescued buildings from the humble 18thC shepherd's hut to atmospheric 'Bayleaf', a fine 15thC timber-framed hall-house from Chiddingstone in Kent which is heated by an open fire in winter months. The buildings which include houses, barns, agricultural buildings, rural craft workshops and an old village school have been re-erected, preserved and carefully sited as a reminder of a past way of life. Many of the buildings contain artefacts and as it's very much a continuous project, you can be sure there's always something new to see.

All the buildings have an interest of their own but a few are singled out here to give you some idea of what you will find. There are some toll houses which once stood on turnpike roads to collect tolls from passing traffic; the Market Hall from Titchfield in Hampshire with stairs leading down to the 'cage' or lock-up for offenders; and the Smithy from Southwater, Sussex, a rough and ready building used by the village blacksmith. Drawings and old tools of the trade illustrate the smith's work in the forge which involved not only shoeing horses but also making and repairing farming implements and equipment. A building of special interest is the watermill from Lurgashall in Sussex. The old mill, parts of which date back to the 17thC, finished its working life in the 1930s but has now been restored and once again grinds corn for flour which you can sample for yourself. The flour, biscuits and a recipe book are on sale both at the mill and in the museum shop.

The museum holds a series of events and exhibitions throughout the main season, such as demonstrations of heavy horses at work and ploughing with vintage tractors. You may like to time your visit to coincide with one of their special activities, so it is a good idea to telephone first to get the relevant information.

Practical details

Weald and Downland Open Air Museum, Singleton, Chichester, West Sussex. (024 363) 348.

Open Apr–Oct   Nov–Mar 11.00–16.00
11.00–17.00 Mon–Sun;   Wed, Sun & Bank Hols.

Admission charge.
Disabled facilities limited access.
Other facilities free parking, café and picnic facilities, toilets, shop.
Rail Victoria to Chichester (1hr 40mins) and then bus (6 miles).

Coach National Express Victoria direct (2hrs 30mins).
Nearby Butlin's Southcoast World (10 miles), Goodwood (6 miles), Wildfowl Trust, Arundel (11 miles).

TREAT!

If you're planning a trip to the open air museum in summer, then close by and well worth visiting are West Dean Gardens with garden centre attached. You'll find 30 acres (12.2ha) of gardens with a huge range of trees and shrubs and there's also a wild garden, pergola and lovely walled garden which has recently been restored. If you find gardening a chore and think mowing the lawn is a back-breaking job, take a look at the collection of antique lawn mowers and other tools and implements. You'll be in for quite a surprise!

West Dean Gardens, Singleton. (024 363) 303. Open Apr–Sep 11.00–18.00 (last admission 17.00). Charge.

TREAT!

WESTONBIRT ARBORETUM
95 miles S

The arboretum is recognised as one of the finest and largest collections of trees and shrubs in the world. Indeed, the statistics are quite staggering – some 14,000 trees and shrubs, rare and common, set along 17 miles of beautiful paths and glades. The arboretum is noted for the vivid colour of the autumn foliage when the Acer Glade is a showcase of autumnal splendour, but it provides a changing feast of colour and interest whatever the season. The winter flowering shrubs give way to the resplendent camellia and magnolia in early spring, then a little later come the brilliant colours of rhododendrons and azaleas and during the summer months there are the glorious hibiscus and hydrangeas.

Westonbirt Arboretum is so huge you couldn't possibly hope to explore it all in a week, let alone a day, so it's worth calling into the Visitor Centre as soon as you arrive. Displays highlight the main features and describe the history of the arboretum since its foundation in 1929 and its role today as a research establishment. The staff are knowledgeable and friendly and will be happy to advise on what you should see for the time of year. The best way to explore the arboretum is by following one of the special waymarked routes. These trails are of varying lengths and take in different points of interest along the way. Themes include the Heritage Trail, the Autumn Colour Trail, the Silk Wood Trail, and Sir George's Glade – a short, circular trail for less able visitors. Information boards at the various 'tree stops' give details such as origin, use and environmental needs plus some fascinating titbits: did you know, for example, that the Turks used the fruit of the horse-chestnut as a drug to cure coughs in horses – hence the name horse-chestnut!

The paths do tend to get rather muddy underfoot so go prepared – sturdy shoes or wellington boots are the dress of the day. After your energetic walk there are refreshments on sale to set you up for the journey home. Situated just beside the Visitor Centre is the tea pavilion which has benches outside and is a peaceful spot to enjoy a snack and admire the scenic views across Silk Wood and the Down Plantation.

Practical details

Westonbirt Arboretum, Tetbury, Glos. (0666) 88220.

Open arboretum all year 10.00–20.00 Mon–Sun. Visitor Centre Apr–mid	Nov 10.00–17.00 Mon–Sun. *Admission* charge.

Disabled facilities all gravel paths are suitable for wheelchairs but quality of tracks varies.
Other facilities car park, toilets, café and picnic area, shop.

No public transport
Nearby Avebury (25 miles), Bath (20 miles), Cotswold Wild Life Park (26 miles).

TREAT!

For a wonderful selection of freshly made bar food, make for the Gentle Gardener at Tetbury, just 3½ miles east of the arboretum. This friendly pub and wine bar has a nice garden, as you might expect from the name, and also has a fascinating menu, so save some time just to drool over it before ordering. Real ale fans will also appreciate the selection of beer on hand-pump and there are rooms available if you're looking for somewhere to stay.

The Gentle Gardener, 23 Long St. (0666) 52884.

TREAT!

WHITBREAD HOP FARM
40 miles SE

A group of traditional Victorian white-topped oast houses act as perfect signposts, beckoning visitors to the hop farm. It's a working farm, providing hops for the Whitbread brewery, and visitors can see the hops being grown and picked. Until as recently as 1968, when machines took over the job, hop-pickers would come for a working holiday in September and October to help with the harvest. The stimulating mixture of holiday and working atmosphere still prevails, making it the ideal setting for a day out to learn more about the history of hops and hop-picking. It's a subject that

Whitbread Hop Farm

seems to inspire school-age children with a host of intelligent questions; adults and children alike can learn a lot from the answers given by well-informed guides and teachers.

There are two museums on the site. The first tells the story of hops from Roman days when they were eaten as we eat asparagus tips, through the heyday of hop growing in Victorian times, plus the customs, traditions and superstitions. History is brought right up to date with explanations and demonstrations of the methods of planting and maintaining a hop garden, then the harvesting, drying and pressing into large 75-kilo 'pockets' ready to be taken to Whitbread breweries. The second, the Whitbread Farm Museum, has displays of rural crafts and the old tools that would have been used by rural tradesmen including the wheelwright, waggoner, blacksmith, thatcher, basket-maker and hedger.

The farm is also the training ground and retirement and holiday home for the mighty Whitbread Shires that pull barrel-laden drays through the City of London. There's no sign of any barrels of beer on the farm, or any taste of the contents. However, it's tonic enough just to see the huge but gentle horses, enjoying the freedom of the fields, their manes and tails flowing gracefully in the wind. And to ensure a full day of both education and entertainment, there are some good walks around the farm with a nature trail to the River Medway, craft workshops, a grassy picnic area and a playground for younger children.

Practical details

Whitbread Hop Farm, Beltring, Paddock Wood, Kent. (0622) 872068.

Open Apr–Oct 10.00–17.30 (last entry 17.00) Tue–Sun & Bank Hol Mons.
Admission charge.
Disabled facilities limited access (contact in advance).
Other facilities free car park, toilets, gift shop, café and picnic area, play area for children.

Rail Charing Cross to Beltring (55mins) then 10-minute walk.
Nearby Hever (16 miles), Knole (14 miles), Penshurst Vineyards (12 miles).

TREAT!

To make it a real day out on the farm, combine your visit to the hop farm with meeting some rare breeds of farm animals at Great Hollanden Farm. There's also a pick-your-own centre for soft fruit and vegetables, and a shop selling fresh produce.

Hollanden Rare Farm Animals, Mill Lane, Hildenborough, Nr Sevenoaks. (0732) 832276. Shop and pick-your-own centre open Apr–mid Oct 09.00–18.00 Mon–Sun; rare breeds and park open Apr–mid Oct 11.30–17.00 Mon–Sun. Charge.

TREAT!

THE WILDFOWL TRUST, ARUNDEL
60 miles S

Swan Lake is a magnificent sight in early January. Here wintering flocks of wild ducks join the tame birds to squabble over the afternoon feed. The fast yet graceful movements of the wildfowl make a colourful, action-packed scene and a fascinating start to a visit to this reserve, the seventh and latest of the wildfowl centres founded by Sir Peter Scott.

The reserve occupies over 60 acres (24.3ha) of wetlands between the River Arun and Swanbourne Lake and is set in a beautiful spot. The historic battlements of Arundel Castle look down on the landscaped lakes and meadows, sheltered by the wooded hillside of Offham Hanger, and provide a truly picturesque backdrop. There's a permanent collection of around 1200 feathered inhabitants here; tame and wild, native and foreign, common and rare, and these are joined by many more migrating wildfowl especially during the winter months. To find out more about the ducks, geese, swans and wild birds you're likely to see, it's worth taking a look at the exhibition in the entrance building which explains about the work, aims and history of the reserve and the Wildfowl Trust.

The large picture windows in the entrance building act as an indoor viewing gallery of the reserve. As you'll see, there isn't a vast area to cover, and you're free to wander as you wish among the friendly ducks. If you can concentrate long enough to read them against the background noise of chirping, cheeping and whistling, information boards give details of the different species so you know with whom you're mixing. You may, however, prefer to buy (at a nominal price) the trail leaflet that guides you along a recommended route, giving an account of the wildfowl and their habits, and a description of the environment along the way. Of particular interest are the observation hides which offer a rare chance to watch wild, native species in their natural habitat; a map inside each one shows what you should look out for. But be warned, you need patience to be a bird-watcher and it may well be some time, if at all, before you make any significant sightings of these shy birds.

Practical details

The Wildfowl Trust, Mill Road, Arundel, West Sussex. (0903) 883355.

Open Apr–Oct 09.30–18.00 Mon–Sun; Nov–Mar 09.30–17.00 Mon–Sun. Closed Christmas Day.
Admission charge.
Disabled facilities good access including the use of free wheelchairs.
Other facilities free car park, toilets, gift shop, restaurant (with lovely views over the reserve), cinema, guided walks. No dogs allowed.

Rail Victoria to Arundel (1hr 20mins), then a short walk.
Coach National Express Victoria to Bognor Regis (3hrs), then train to Arundel (10mins).
Nearby Butlin's Southcoast World (15 miles), Goodwood (12 miles), South Downs Way (17 miles), Weald and Downland Open Air Museum (11 miles).

TREAT!

Arundel is a quaint market town with narrow streets, olde-worlde tea-houses and antique shops that you can spend hours browsing around. The dominating feature, however, is Arundel Castle, set in 1000 acres (405ha) of lovely parkland. The castle, built in the 12thC and rich in English history, boasts many fine paintings including works by Reynolds and Gainsborough, and a collection of furniture dating back to the 16thC.

Arundel Castle, Arundel. (0903) 883136/882173. Open Apr–Oct 13.00 (12.00 Jun–Aug & Bank Hols)–17.00 (last entry 16.00) Sun–Fri. Closed Sat. Charge.

TREAT!

WIMPOLE HALL AND HOME FARM
53 miles N

The hall is grand and sumptuous; the combined efforts
over the years of such celebrated architects as James
Gibbs, Henry Flitcroft, Sir James Thornhill and Sir
John Soane. Its setting in 300 acres (121.5ha) of parkland is perhaps even more impressive, created in
changing styles by the leading landscape gardeners of
their time: Charles Bridgeman, Capability Brown and
Humphrey Repton. And yet there's nothing stately or
formal about Wimpole. Indeed, it's a tribute to the
talents of these great men of the past and to the friendly
staff of today that there's such a relaxed, comfortable
feel to the place. Local National Trust members use
the tea rooms as a favourite café, enjoying excellent
tea and cakes with a view over the surrounding gardens; even children never tire of Wimpole.

The sense of space hits you immediately because it's
a long two-mile drive through parkland to the Kendall
Stable Block where you buy tickets and leave the car.
The park is open from dawn to dusk and free for
everyone to enjoy, with waymarked walks leading you
into some gloriously wild and wooded areas, but you
must pay to see the hall and Home Farm. Call first at
the exhibition in the Tack and Harness Room in the
stable block which shows the development of Wimpole
from its days as a medieval park with moated manor
house, to today's landscaped park and gardens with the
splendid 18thC mansion. The displays certainly give
you something to think about as you walk the short
distance to the hall.

Wimpole Hall is richly decorated; the rooms intimate and interesting with a lovely 'lived-in' atmosphere. Soane's dramatic Yellow Drawing Room and
the Chapel with its surprising baroque interior are
particularly noteworthy. The hall had a succession of
owners throughout its history and slowly fell into dis-

repair before Mrs Elsie Bambridge, daughter of Rudyard Kipling, bought it, spent 40 years refurbishing it and then left the whole estate to the National Trust on her death in 1976. Her study is lined with her much-loved collection of 19thC portraits.

Wimpole's Home Farm can be reached in one of two ways: you can take either a leisurely walk from the hall through the gardens, or a rather bumpy ride in a cart pulled by the estate's two Suffolk Punches. The cart leaves at regular intervals from the stable block. Home Farm was built in the late 18thC and became famous for advanced methods of agriculture. The thatched farm buildings, designed by Soane, still stand today and the Great Barn is home to a museum of farming methods and equipment. Today a variety of different animals including many rare breeds of sheep, cattle, pigs and poultry live on the farm. There's also a children's corner where they can handle the smaller animals, and explanation boards full of facts. Did you know, for example, that Portland Sheep were so named because they supposedly swam ashore from the wrecked Spanish Armada to the Dorset Coast near the Isle of Portland? If you are interested in finding out more about the farm a video is shown three times a day, while the staff are always on hand to help.

Practical details

Wimpole Hall, Park and Home Farm, Arrington, Nr Royston, Herts. (0223) 207257.

Open hall and gardens: Apr–Oct 13.00–17.00 Tue–Thur, Sat & Sun, 11.00–17.00 Bank Hol Mons. Home Farm: Apr–Oct 10.30–17.00 on same days as hall. *Admission* charge (National Trust). *Disabled facilities* wheelchairs and special access available on request. No access to upper floor of hall and park unsuitable. *Other facilities* free car park, toilets (including disabled), large gift shop, café and picnic areas, special events. Dogs not welcome, except guide dogs. *Rail* King's Cross to Shepreth (50mins) or

Royston (55mins) and
then taxi (5/6 miles).
Coach National Express
Victoria to Cambridge
(1hr 50mins) then local
bus (20mins) to Arrington.
Nearby Audley End (12
miles), Cambridge (14
miles), Knebworth (16
miles).

TREAT!

It's well worth making a slight detour on your way
to or from Wimpole to stop at the Chequers Inn in
Fowlmere. The famous diarist Samuel Pepys dined
here on 'breast of roasted veal' in 1660, and today
you can still enjoy tasty meals and snacks. Don't
miss the wonderfully rich ice-cream.

The Chequers Inn, Fowlmere, Cambs. (076382)
369.

TREAT!

WINCHESTER
65 miles SW

Winchester was the capital of England for four hundred years between the reigns of Alfred the Great and
Edward I so, as you might expect, the city is full of
historic interest. The main attractions are within easy
walking distance of each other and can either be visited
independently or on one of the guided tours which
leave from the Tourist Information Centre.

Winchester is perhaps best known for its cathedral
which dates from 1079. It was for many years the
largest in the world and is still only exceeded in length
by St Peter's in Rome and the new Anglican Cathedral
in Liverpool. Among its many treasures are Jane
Austen's tomb; the font in which the infant king,
Henry III, was baptised; the chair which Mary Tudor
used when she was married to Phillip II of Spain; and

the statue of William Walker the Diver who is said to have saved the cathedral from collapse with his own two hands. (He worked underwater for four hours a day for five and a half years rebuilding the foundations which had collapsed after the local authority changed the water level at the beginning of this century.)

Within the Cathedral Close is the Pilgrims' School which provides the choristers for the cathedral and whose Great Hall has a wonderful example of a hammer-beam roof. Just outside the close on the south side is Wolvesey Castle, the ruins of a 12thC palace built by Henri de Blois for himself and later Bishops of Winchester. And nearby is Winchester College founded by another bishop, William of Wykeham, in 1382. The college is probably the last in England to require all its pupils to take Latin up to GCSE level and is also known for the unique brand of football, played during the Easter term, which often confuses spectators. A 15-minute walk from the close brings you to another Great Hall which is the only part left standing of the medieval castle built by Henry III. It houses the famous Round Table, inscribed with the names of the legendary King Arthur and his knights, which was carved in about 1280 and painted in its present form in the 1530s. A rather longer walk of about 20–25

St Cross Hospital

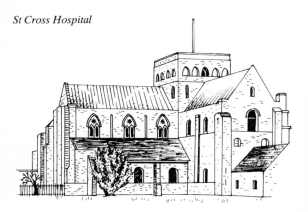

minutes will take you through the Water Meadows bordering the River Itchen to St Cross, the oldest charitable institution in Britain. It was set up in 1136, again by Henri de Blois, to house 13 men who had fallen on hard times and was extended by Cardinal Beaufort to accommodate a further 24 men who were also needy but who were required to have a smattering of education. All the men wore uniforms: the former dressed in black gowns and flat black hats, and the latter in maroon gowns and hats, and the brethren who live at the hospital today can still be seen wearing their uniforms around the city. Another tradition that lingers on is the Travellers' Dole which you can get on request from the Porter's Lodge. This tiny glass of beer and triangle of bread commemorates the bygone days when the first 100 persons to call at St Cross each day would be provided with a quart of ale and half a quartern loaf.

Practical details

Tourist Information Centre, Guildhall, Broadway. (0962) 840222. Open May–Sep 09.30–18.00 Mon–Sat, 14.00–17.00 Sun; Oct–Apr 09.30–17.00 Mon–Sat, closed Sun.

Tours May–mid Oct 10.30 & 14.30 Mon–Sat, 15.00 Sun; mid Oct–end Apr 10.30 Sat. Charge.
Hospital of St Cross, St Cross St. (0962) 51375. Open Apr–Sep 09.00–12.30, 14.00–17.00 Mon–Sun; Oct–Mar 10.30–12.30, 14.00–15.30 Mon–Sun. Charge.
Pilgrims Hall, Cathedral Close. (0962) 54189. Open when not in daily use by the school. Free.
Winchester Cathedral, Cathedral Close. (0962)

53137. Open 07.30–18.30 Mon–Sun. Tours Apr–Oct 11.00 & 15.00 Mon–Sun. Free but donation suggested.
Winchester College, College St. (0962) 64242. Open Apr–Sep 10.00–18.00 Mon–Sat, 14.00–18.00 Sun; Oct–Mar 10.00–16.00 Mon–Sat, 14.00–16.00 Sun. Free but charge for guided tour.
Wolvesey Castle, College St. (0962) 54766. Open Apr–Sep 09.30–20.30

Mon–Sat, 14.00–18.30
Sun. Closed 13.00–14.00
Mon–Sat. Charge.
Rail Waterloo to
Winchester (1hr).
Coach National Express
Victoria to Winchester
(2hrs).

Nearby Broadlands (10
miles), Hawk
Conservancy (16 miles),
Salisbury (23 miles).

┌ *TREAT!* ─────────────────

The Wykeham Arms is an attractive 18thC hostelry and coaching inn conveniently situated between the cathedral and the college. Named 'Pub of the Year' in 1987 by Egon Ronay, it serves a wide range of foods cooked by a cordon bleu chef. There's a welcoming log fire in the winter and a garden for summer visitors.

The Wykeham Arms, 75 Kingsgate St. (0962) 53834.

───────────────── *TREAT!* ┘

WINDSOR CASTLE AND THE GREAT PARK
20 miles W

There's usually a huddle of tourists waiting expectantly outside Cambridge Gate at the park end of Park Street. This is the entrance used by the Royal Family on their frequent visits to this popular castle so there's always hope of spotting a royal face. The castle acts like a magnet to visitors as it looms majestically over Windsor town, surrounded by an air of fairytale magic. Originally built by William the Conqueror, it holds the title as the oldest and largest inhabited castle in the world. It covers some 13 acres (5.3ha) in total. Outside, the precincts are open to the public, except on Garter Day in June, free of charge. A good time to visit is 11.00 for the spectacle of the Changing of the Guard which takes place on most days throughout the year. However, it's inside that the treasures are to be found. And they're so spectacular they really do have to be seen to be believed – the sumptuous State Apartments still used by the Queen; the rich architecture of St George's Chapel, burial place of ten monarchs including King Henry VIII; the distinctive Curfew Tower which houses the eight Chapel bells; Queen Mary's Dolls' House designed by Sir Edwin Lutyens with such perfect detailing, and much, much more.

The Long Walk is a three-mile avenue of trees stretching from the castle to the Copper Horse, a statue of George III on horseback erected in 1831. It's along here that the Queen drives during Royal Ascot Week on her way to the racecourse. Popular with joggers, dog-walkers, and even horse-drawn carriages that trot along it, the avenue is a lovely place for a leisurely stroll away from the summertime crowds, or a brisk walk on a cold winter's day. If the thought of a three-mile hike seems daunting, then rest assured, the views from the Copper Horse are ample reward. Do take your binoculars to enjoy them to the full. From the top of Snow Hill, the magnificent Great Park stretches before you – some 4800 acres (1944ha) of woodland, farms and open fields which were once part of a large royal hunting forest and are now a wonderful walking ground. As you stand with your back to Windsor Castle, the meadows of Runnymede lie to your right. It was here that King John put his seal on the famous Magna Carta in 1215. In front of you, are the Savill Garden, 35 acres (14.2ha) of woodland, and Valley Gardens, 400 acres (162ha) where rhododendrons, camellias and magnolias bloom in season, on the banks of Virginia Water. This artificial lake, created from marshy streams in the mid 18thC, is surrounded by wooded walks – an outing to remember for another day. Between the Savill Garden and Valley Gardens is Smith's Lawn, where polo matches are played most weekends during the summer months and equestrian events held throughout the year (the Tourist Information Centre will provide all the details).

Refreshed by the views, it is now time to return with the castle always ahead beckoning you back to historic Royal Windsor, with its cobbled streets and quality shops, tea rooms and restaurants. It's well worth visiting the Royalty and Empire Exhibition which depicts 60 years of British history in models, tableaux and a theatre show.

Practical details

Tourist Information Centre, Central Station. (0753) 852010. Open Apr–Oct 09.30–18.30 Mon–Sat, 10.00–18.30 Sun; Nov–Mar 09.30–17.30 Mon–Sat, 10.00–16.00 Sun.

Royalty and Empire Exhibition, Windsor and Eton Central Railway Station. (0753) 57837. *Savill Garden and Valley Gardens*, Crown Estate Office, The Great Park. (0753) 860222. Savill Garden open Mar–24 Dec 10.00–19.00 (or dusk if earlier) Mon–Sun. Charge. Valley Gardens open at all times. Free. *Windsor Castle*. (0753) 868286. Opening times vary depending on the movements of the Royal Family and ceremonial occasions, so check with the Castle Information Office. Charge for interior. *Rail* Paddington to Windsor (35mins). Waterloo to Windsor (47mins). *Coach* Green Line Victoria to Windsor (1hr 15mins). *Nearby* Bekonscot Model Village (10 miles), Chessington World of Adventures (16 miles), Thorpe Park (20 miles).

TREAT!

No trip to Windsor would be complete without a traditional English tea so indulge yourself in the tea served at the Castle Hotel. Built in the late 17thC as a Posting Inn, you can't miss its large Georgian frontage which seems to dominate the

High Street. The menu includes a simple cream tea with scones and clotted cream or, if you really want to treat yourself, there's a set tea which includes a selection of mouth-watering gateaux.

The Castle Hotel, High St. (0753) 851011. Afternoon tea served 15.00–17.30 Mon–Sun.

TREAT!

WINDSURFING – A BEGINNER'S COURSE
160 miles S

At the Weymouth Sailing Centre you can take the Royal Yachting Association Boardsailing Award. Designed for beginners, it lasts eight hours. If you're fit you can do the course in one day, but if you think your muscles are likely to ache after a few hours strenuous exercise (and the experts at the centre find that most people's do), then you may opt to spread your course over several sessions – the flexibility offered by this centre is one of its definite pluses.

The RYA course covers theory, rigging, safety and self-rescue techniques as well as the physical activity of sailing. However, for a beginner the day begins on a simulator. The simulator is a fixed board on dry land. For the expert, hoisting the mast and heavy sail on a simulator is a simple exercise and the tanned instructor demonstrates the various manoeuvres with grace and ease. For the beginner, though, the whole process is usually one large embarrassing wobble! It comes as a surprise, therefore, that after about 30 minutes most people do seem to master the basic principles of windsurfing and it is time then to squeeze into a wet suit and plunge into the water. Once in the sea, and no matter what size the waves, the sailboard seems enormous and uncontrollable but there are instructors, safely ensconced in canoes, to shout advice or rescue any novice who drifts too far from the shore. An hour or so later comes the first experience of actually sailing. Once balanced, it doesn't seem such a difficult thing after all – so long as the wind is behind you. However, when a worried instructor shouts that it's time to turn and tack into the wind most learners panic, fall into the water, and end up walking to the beach dragging their boards behind them.

By the end of the course the average learner is equipped with the rudiments of windsurfing and you should be able to rig your own board and sail reasonably competently in a light wind. You should also be able to gossip with confidence to other new sailboard enthusiasts!

Practical details

Weymouth Sailing Centre, Sandsfoot Beach, Old Castle Rd, Weymouth, Dorset. (0305) 776549.

Open 09.00–17.00 Mon–Sun.
Admission charge. Courses must be booked in advance. Minimum age for unaccompanied children is 8.
Disabled facilities difficult for disabled people but not impossible. Ring for advice.
Other facilities café, barbecue, picnicking on beach, car park, hot showers (free), bar, toilets, shop.

Rail Victoria to Weymouth (2hrs 30mins).
Coach National Express Victoria to Weymouth (summer only, 3hrs).
Nearby Poole (25 miles).
Note wet suit, bouyancy aid and sailboard provided but you'll need to bring a pair of old trainers (which will get wet), a swimming costume and a towel. It's also a good idea to have some warm clothes for afterwards.

TREAT!

A walk along nearby Chesil Beach should not be missed. This dramatic pebble shoreline is some ten miles long. At the end of the beach nearest the sailing centre you can see the Isle of Portland which

shelters Weymouth Harbour. On this rocky
plateau, which is joined to the mainland by a
narrow causeway of shingle, stands Portland
Castle, one of Henry VIII's coastal defences.

TREAT!

WISLEY GARDEN
30 miles SW

The Royal Horticultural Society's Garden at Wisley is
a must for every gardening enthusiast. Whenever you
visit there's something to catch the eye – spectacular
herbaceous borders in summer; the subtle hues of the
Heather Garden on a bright autumn day; the golden
drifts of *Narcissus Cyclamineus* which carpet the floor
of the Wild Garden, and the bright daffodils in the
Alpine Meadow in the springtime. Then there are the
glasshouses, the new introductions of bush and climb-
ing roses, a herb garden, model gardens, a fruit collection and the famous Rock Garden which is a mass of
colour during April and May. It's hard to know where
to begin your tour.

The first plantings were made at Wisley in 1878.
Initially, there were only about 6 acres (2.43ha) under
cultivation, centred mainly around the Wild Garden.
Today, its 240 acres (97.2ha) are renowned throughout
the world and Wisley is recognised as an important
centre for horticultural practice. One of the main
functions of the garden is the trial of new varieties of
flowers and vegetables so do make sure you visit
Portsmouth Field, the main trial area. Advice and help
on horticultural problems is another part of its work
and the model gardens are an inspiration for all green-
fingered amateurs, showing some of the secrets of
garden layout and planning. The model fruit and
vegetable gardens demonstrate how even very small
areas can be cultivated. And there's a plot of land set

aside to show suitable garden features and helpful gardening techniques for disabled and elderly people.

There's such a wide range of plants at Wisley that it's tempting to take cuttings but leave your clippers at home – it's strictly forbidden to take any plant materials from the garden. However, if you're looking for a souvenir of your visit then head for the Plant Sales Area by the main entrance where you can buy plants, including many unusual ones, in containers. Nearby is the Information Centre with books and goods on a gardening theme.

Practical details

Royal Horticultural Society's Garden, Wisley, Woking, Surrey. (0483) 224234.

Open Feb–Oct 10.00–19.00 (or dusk if earlier) Mon–Sat, 14.00–19.00 Sun; Nov–Jan 10.00–16.30 Mon–Sat, 14.00–16.30 Sun. Closed Christmas Day. Sun mornings reserved for members. *Admission* charge. *Disabled facilities* including toilets. Specially prepared route for wheelchairs. *Other facilities* free car park, toilets, café, licensed restaurant, picnic area near the car park, Information Centre and shop. Demonstrations on horticultural subjects and techniques given throughout the year. No dogs (except guide dogs) allowed. *Rail* Waterloo to Esher (25mins) and then Green Line. Waterloo to West Byfleet (40mins) and then taxi. *Coach* Green Line Oxford Street direct (1hr 30mins). *Nearby* Birdworld (20 miles), Chessington World of Adventures (12 miles), Loseley House (8 miles), Thorpe Park (10 miles).

TREAT!

Garden lovers will appreciate the neat and well-kept garden of the Cricketers on Downside Common. Delightful in the summer when you can enjoy snacks on the tables outside, this olde-worlde pub is equally inviting in the winter when a log fire adds

to the atmosphere. There's a good selection of
reasonably priced food at the bar and a restaurant
serving more substantial meals.

The Cricketers, Downside Common. (0932)
62105.

_____ *TREAT!*

WOBURN ABBEY AND WOBURN WILD ANIMAL KINGDOM
44 miles NW

Firstly, don't make the mistake of thinking that
Woburn Abbey and Woburn Wild Animal Kingdom
are one and the same – they're not. Although situated
in the same parkland they are run separately and you
have to pay separately to visit each one. Secondly, if
you go to the abbey expecting to see an ancient monas-
tery, you are in for a surprise. Although built on the
site of a Cistercian settlement founded in 1145, today's
building dates mainly from the 18thC with some earlier
Jacobean features.

The treasures on view inside the abbey are both
impressive and important. They include the highly
acclaimed Armada Portrait of Elizabeth I; a compel-
ling image of the Queen as Empress, her hand on a
globe and background scenes of the Spanish fleet being
attacked by Drake's fire-ships. Other portraits may be
seen as you ascend the cantilevered Grand Staircase,
thought to be the design of Henry Flitcroft. There's a
portrait of the fourth Earl of Bedford by Van Dyck,
and of the third Countess of Bedford, attributed to
John de Critz.

Porcelain is also an important feature to be enjoyed
at Woburn. Look out for the cabinet which contains

the 'forget-me-not' (19thC Meissen) collection. Down in the crypt there's an eye-catching display of 17thC Japanese porcelain and some interesting Wedgwood caneware (c1820). Dominating the crypt, however, is a draped pavilion housing the Sèvres dinner service which was presented to the fourth Duchess by Louis XV, in appreciation of her husband's role in negotiating the Treaty of Paris in 1763.

There are many stunning rooms on show including the Yellow Drawing Room (used by Prince Albert, during his stay in 1841, as a sitting room); Queen Victoria's Bedroom and Sitting Room; the State Room and State Dining Room; the Reynolds Room; and the Canaletto Room (part of the Private Apartments). The most intriguing room of all is the Grotto – a folly probably built between 1619–41. Its stonework is elaborately carved to resemble seaweed and stalactites, inlaid with ormer shells from the Channel Islands, and mussel shells. The 18thC furniture is carved in the shape of sea shells with dolphins supporting the seats and table tops.

A few minutes' drive from the abbey, through the 3000-acre (1215ha) Deer Park, brings you to Woburn Wild Animal Kingdom. Here a winding route passes through a number of enclosures containing lions, tigers, monkeys, bears, wolves, or rhinos where *you* provide the animals with some entertainment.

Monkeys in particular seem to enjoy their visitors, but be warned – a monkey's idea of fun is pulling a wind-screen wiper off a car. At the end of the Safari Trail there's a leisure park where you can see parrot and sea-lion shows and watch an elephant display. There's also a cabin-lift 'Sky Ride' (lasts about 15 minutes) above some of the prettier areas of the park. For the young there's a pets corner, and for the young at heart there's a colourful carousel. Finally, have a go on the 60ft (18.3m) high 'Rainbow': if the screams of those already on board don't frighten you away!

Practical details

Woburn Abbey and Woburn Wild Animal Kingdom, Woburn, Beds. (0525) 290666.

Open Abbey Jan–Mar 11.00–16.00 (last admission) Sat & Sun; Apr–Oct 11.00–17.00 (last admission) Mon–Sat, 11.30–17.30 (last admission) Sun. Closed Nov & Dec. Deer Park open Jan–Mar 10.30–dusk Sat & Sun; Apr–Oct 10.00–dusk Mon–Sat, 10.00–17.45 Sun. Closed Nov & Dec. Wild Animal Kingdom open mid Mar–Oct 10.00–17.00 Mon–Sun.
Admission separate charge for Abbey and Animal Kingdom. Extra charge for Private Apartments.
Disabled facilities access good (ie inside a car) to Deer Park and Animal Kingdom; very limited access to abbey.
Other facilities Abbey: car park, self-service restaurant, antiques centre (admission charge), picnic area, gift shop. Animal Kingdom: car park, ghost train (free), carousel (free), Sky Ride (free), animal displays (free), picnic area, toilets, gift shop, self-service restaurant, boating lake (free).
Rail Euston to Leighton Buzzard (45mins) or Bletchley (50mins), or St Pancras to Flitwick (1hr) and then taxi (6–7 miles).
Coach Green Line Victoria to Woburn Abbey (2hrs).
Note Wild Animal Kingdom not accessible by public transport. You must have a car to visit the safari park.
Nearby Knebworth (25 miles), Shuttleworth Collection (25 miles), Waterways Museum, Towcester (24 miles).

TREAT!

The Bell Inn in Woburn is an unusual pub in that it caters for eaters rather than drinkers. Of course you can get a good pint, but the emphasis is definitely on food. Here you can enjoy a meal in the restaurant or a plate of reasonably priced food in the bar. And if the sun shines you can eat in the small, sheltered, patio beer garden.

The Bell Inn, 21 Bedford St. (0525) 290 280.

TREAT!

INDEX

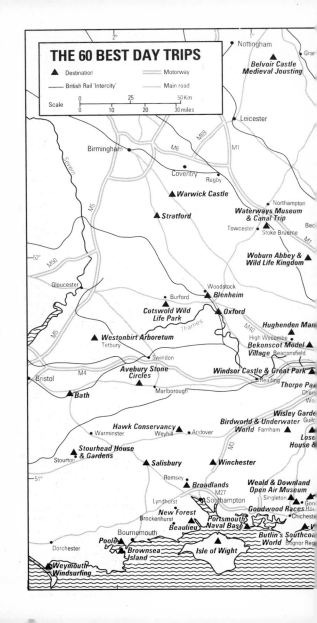

THE 60 BEST DAY TRIPS

▲ Destination   ▬▬ Motorway

── British Rail 'Intercity'   ── Main road

Scale   0   25   50 Km

0   10   20   30 miles

Nottingham

Grar

▲ **Belvoir Castle**
Medieval Jousting

Leicester

Birmingham

M6

M69

M1

Coventry

Rugby

▲ **Warwick Castle**

Northampton

▲ **Stratford**

Waterways Museum
& Canal Trip

Towcester • Stoke Bruerne

Bed

M1

▲ **Woburn Abbey &**
Wild Life Kingdom

Gloucester

M50

Woodstock

Burford

▲ **Blenheim**

Cotswold Wild
Life Park

▲ **Oxford**

Thames

▲ **Hughenden Man**

High Wycombe

M40

▲ **Westonbirt Arboretum**

Tetbury

Bekonscot Model ▲
Village Beaconsfield

Swindon

M5

▲ **Avebury Stone**
Circles

M4

Windsor Castle & Great Park ▲

Reading

Bristol

Marlborough

Thorpe Pa

▲ **Bath**

Cher

Wo

Wisley Garde

Hawk Conservancy ▲

Birdworld & Underwater ▲
World Farnham

Guil

Warminster

Weyhill

• Andover

M3

▲
Lose
House &

▲ **Stourhead House**
& Gardens

Stourton

▲ **Salisbury**

▲ **Winchester**

Romsey

▲ **Broadlands**

Weald & Downland
Open Air Museum

M27

Singleton ▲ ▲ Go

Lyndhurst

▲ Southampton

Goodwood Races Ho

New Forest

Brockenhurst

Portsmouth

Beaulieu

Naval Base

• Chichest

Bournemouth

Butlin's Southcoa ▲
World Bognor Reg

Poole

▲

Dorchester

▲ **Brownsea**
Island

Isle of Wight

~~**Weymouth**~~
~~**Windsurfing**~~

King's Lynn

Peterborough

Huntingdon
afham Water

▲ Norwich

Great
Yarmouth

▲ Ely Cathedral

Newmarket
National Horseracing
Museum & Equine Tour

▲ Cambridge Colleges
Arrington
▲ Wimpole Hall & Home Farm

Shuttleworth Collection
eswade • Royston
• Saffron Walden

A1(M)
Audley End

orth House,
s & Park
• Knebworth

M11

Ipswich

▲ Hatfield House

ans

Epping •

▲ Hobbs Cross
Open Farm

Southend-on-Sea

M25

ngton World
dventures

M20

M2

▲ Canterbury

Knole
Sevenoaks

Maidstone

▲ Leeds Castle

Hever Castle ▲
& Gardens

▲ Whitbread Hop Farm
• Beltring
Paddock Wood   Ashford •

M20

Edenbridge

M23

Penshurst
Vineyards

• Tenterden

Dover

Folkestone

l Railway ▲
Park Station
owns
y
amber
n

▲ Brighton

Uckfield

Battle Abbey
& Battlefield

Drusillas
Zoo
Alfriston

Lewes

Great Dixter House
▲ & Gardens Northiam
▲ Rye
Winchelsea

Hastings

Boulogne ▲

F R A N C E

NICHOLSON

THE BEST IN LONDON

NEW £3.50

NICHOLSON

LOOKING *Good* IN LONDON

The HAIR, BEAUTY, FASHION AND FITNESS GUIDE

£2.95

NICHOLSON

THE GUIDE TO LONDON BY BUS & TUBE

£3.95

NICHOLSON

The London Guide

The most comprehensive guide to London

NEW EDITION

£2.95

NICHOLSON

LONDON

THE GOOD TOUR GUIDE

Visit the 60 most exciting places in town

£3.95

NICHOLSON

LONDON Arts and CULTURAL GUIDE

THEATRE Dance MUSEUMS Music Festivals CINEMA HOUSES Galleries

£3.50

NICHOLSON

LONDON RESTAURANT GUIDE

Over 700 places to eat More than 30 national cuisines

NEW EDITION

£3.50

NICHOLSON

LONDON

GUIDE

£2.

NICHOLSON

LONDON DOCKLANDS MAP

LONDON DOCKLANDS STREET ATLAS & GUIDE

NEW LARGE 5 IN

Nicholson publishes a
large range of guide books
covering various aspects of London
life. Whatever your interest you can
rely on Nicholson to give you accurate
up-to-date information in a compact and portable form.